BIG SHOW
tiny budget

BIG SHOW
tiny budget

—

an idea book for every stage designer,

from high school to Broadway,

who wishes he had money to burn

but can't afford a disposable lighter

—

Sean Martin

A Smith and Kraus Book
Published by Smith and Kraus, Inc.
177 Lyme Road, Hanover, NH 03755
www.smithandkraus.com

First Edition: March 2008
Manufactured in the United States of America
10 9 8 7 6 5 4 3 2 1

Book production by Julia Gignoux, Freedom Hill Design
Cover and text design by Kate Mueller, Electric Dragon Productions

Library of Congress Control Number: 2007939329
ISBN: 978-1-57525-569-9

to everyone who ever gave me a chance

—

and to everyone who, despite everything,

turned around and gave me a second chance . . .

—

but most importantly, to the students, teachers, staff,

and parents of Washington County High

Acknowledgments

Not OFTEN DOES ONE GET THE OPPORTUNITY to write about the passions that drive him in this exasperating profession we all love, let alone thank the many folks who helped make that profession possible. So if you'll indulge me . . .

Whatever its ultimate worth, this book would not be in your hands, were it not for, first and foremost, Scott, Susan, and Sydney Price, who went from a client and his wife and daughter to three very dear friends. Scott took a leap of faith in a designer three thousand miles away and gave me the opportunity to play to my heart's content, and it pushed me creatively beyond anything I could have ever dreamed. We've seen each other through really good productions and really bad productions. Whenever I was feeling doubt about my capabilities, Scott was there with a shoulder and an ear, reassuring beyond all measure. I owe you big time, bud. And yes, one of these days we'll do *South Pacific*.

Washington County High School's drama department has a fiercely devoted bunch of parents, some of whom continue to support the school long after their children have graduated. Of all of them, I have to cite Sandra McMaster, whose daughter Laura created Domina in the school's original production of *Forum*. Even after Laura left for college, Mrs. McMaster was still there, making sure costumes were completed and props were secured and opening night parties were arranged.

Also, Mike Quail, Neal Debrecini, and Carla Foster, who were supportive of my absurd midlife crisis to leave a perfectly good career in advertising for something as ridiculous as the theatre. Every year I missed Neal's birthday because I was somewhere on the road, and only rarely did Neal complain loud enough that I could hear. The karaoke nights and the drag shows and That House were buckets of reality-brand ice water, reminders that work—even work you enjoy—is all well and good, but friends are forever.

Randy Riddle, who understands, perhaps more than most, the love-hate relationship with one's work that comes in any creative profession.

Scott Chandler, who wrangled our houseful of cats while I was off on all-night stints animating "God" or weekends away teching Donizetti. You know who loves ya, baby . . .

My professional associates, too many to mention, spanning eight countries and three continents. You folks have given me opportunities beyond any designer's wildest dreams, and I am indeed humbled and proud to call you not only colleagues but friends as well.

Finally, the good people at Smith and Kraus, who surely decided in a moment of madness that this was a book worth publishing. I also have to thank my incomparable editor Kate Mueller, who did her job so well that even I didn't notice how much work she'd done. I hope it meets your expectations and then some.

Contents

Foreword

In THE SUMMER OF 2001, I DECIDED TO SOLICIT the assistance of a professional scenic designer via the Internet for our fledgling high-school theatre program. I had several responses on the job posting, from young designers fresh out of undergrad to those who have drafted from every angle of a proscenium and then some. None of the designers came close in comparison to Sean's talents. I am pleased to say that we have collaborated on every production since *Forum* in 2001 to our most recent productions of *Godspell* and *Scapino* in 2006–2007, and I doubt it'll stop there. For a high-school theatre program with a shoestring budget, Sean has made us look pretty darn good when the lights go up.

Our approach has been to create a clean, polished, aesthetic feel on a tiny stage with a tiny budget. With a thirty-foot proscenium and about twenty-five feet from apron center to the center of the cyclorama (not to mention the closet-size wings), Sean and I have faced many a challenge to turn out major musicals and plays in this space. And we've met every one.

Most of the shows have been built for under five hundred dollars. Seriously. At the same time, they have won awards and have been recognized at one-act play competitions, the Georgia Theatre Conference, and state thespian conferences—all this from a small-town high-school theatre program in central Georgia, on a small stage, and, most importantly, on a small budget! It can be done!

Scott Price
Director, Theatre Department
Washington County High School
Sandersville, Georgia

Let's have some fun!

BENI MONTRESSOR

OK, So What's This Book Really About?

So YOU'VE THOUGHT A LONG TIME ABOUT IT. You really, really, really want to tackle that big-time musical. It has lots of roles, which will keep lots of grandparents happy. The music is available from the licensing house on a rental CD, which means you don't have to deal with the band director. Well, there's one mercy.

But there's all that scenery. And all those costumes. And you don't have all that money. Well, you have some, but nowhere near enough to pull this particular rabbit out of the hat.

But you really want to do this show.

It's not impossible. I swear. You don't have to consign yourself to yet another production of *Grease*. You really can do this show, whatever it is, honest. And it will be riveting. Or charming. Or magical. A one-of-a-kind experience for you and your students. Bear with me, and I'll show you how. First though, a little background. You might as well know whom you're dealing with, right?

My first experience with high-school musical theatre was my high-school alma mater's production of *The Pajama Game*, in which I played All-Purpose Chorus Boy Number 3. My sole line, every night, was "Who's there?"—and I muffed it every night.

Regardless of what the script dictated, our production was performed in front of wine-red velvet curtains. The factory was suggested (if that's the right word) by an array of battered student desks taken from the janitor's storeroom. The company picnic was that old standby, the bare stage. Closing the main curtain served for scenes in offices and hallways. The sole exception was Hernando's Hideaway, which was clearly where our production's limited finances were spent. We constructed three large wagon units, of no apparent design, and painted them in then-trendy op-art-inspired black and white. It was about as Spanish as a french fry. As it turned out, they were onstage for about eight minutes, and then went away, and we were back to wine-red velvets for the rest of the show. The lighting was full up or full down, nothing in between. We had one follow spot that had one setting for edge softness: none. If there was any directorial or scenic concept to any of all of this beyond simple expediency, to this day I have no idea what it might have been. And I'm sure the original creators would have cringed in horror.

With graduation, I moved into the slightly more interesting world of university theatre, where the design goals may have been more ambitious, but the execution was equally dismal. In one adventurous year, my college mounted Sheridan's *The Rivals* and followed it with *You're a Good Man Charlie Brown*. For reasons too improbable to explain, we used more or less the same set for both.

Since those bleak beginnings, I've somehow managed to cobble together a career as a designer. I've never studied stage design formally, save for one undergraduate course. I worked more or less full-time as a graphic designer and illustrator for ten years before making the leap into a more or less full-time theatre career. As such, everything I've learned has been hands-on, from a series of very experienced and talented technical directors who knew how to take my nascent (and sometimes naïve) designs and turn them into something stage-worthy. I consider myself fortunate to have been given the opportunity to work on over two hundred productions, everything from pocket opera in Illinois to a major world premiere in Spain. But there's one factor I can never forget when approaching a new assignment.

Budget. I've worked with six-figure budgets and three-figure budgets. To all of them I've aspired, as any decent designer would, to bring a sense of visual whole, no matter how sprawling the script or complex the director's concept. And yet the one thing I must remember is how much all of this is costing someone.

(OK. When you see something like this, it's just me interrupting myself. That's gonna happen a lot in this book. Please note: this book may be about doing things on the cheap, but it isn't about scenery made from cardboard. While there are books on that very subject—and good ones, I might add—this one is about concept, first and foremost. It assumes that your production has a budget, no matter how small, that will allow substantive materials for whatever the central design key—and something on that shortly—might be. The key's going to have to work overtime, hauling the rest of the production behind it, so you best give it everything you can. Remember what Lawrence and Lee said about costuming Auntie Mame.)

Even the biggest production has finite resources, yet sometimes it seems I work best when I have less money and materials to play with. I'm not sure why this is, but perhaps it's my graphic design training. For example, when designing a billboard, you get three seconds to get someone's attention, so that billboard has to speak fast and loud and efficiently. And so it is with my approach to theatre design, where the set is seen and noted and then, like a good host at a party, quietly recedes into the background so the actors can get on with their job.

But that's only part of it. After all, if the set disappears, what's the point of having one in the first place? (And I'm sure there are many producers who ask that very question on a regular basis.) Why not do everything in front of wine-red velvets—or better, full-stage blacks? Now, sure, like many designers, I like working with black velvets, not because it hides the stage but because of the empty canvas it provides, a void replete with possibility—sometimes too much so. And that makes the choices all the more difficult. In this respect, good theatre design is like writing a haiku, where you have to get the biggest gesture possible out of the least amount of expression. Perhaps it's because such inherent simplicity recalls a simpler time, when the leading lady made her entrance down a staircase, not aboard a hydraulic lift. A time when a single spotlight could match the work of a dozen automated moving lights. A time when the audience could be dazzled by the whole of the production, not just the eye candy—when theatre could be theatre, not a bastardization of a movie.

To that end, one of my favorite clients is Washington County High School in central Georgia whose theatre department is run by a great guy named Scott Price. We met six years ago, when he was looking for someone to design *A Funny Thing Happened on the Way to the Forum* for a state competition, and I was looking for something for my portfolio. I offered to design both set and costumes for free; he accepted my offer; and we have since collaborated on some thirty to thirty-five productions. The stage is nothing special: thirty feet wide, fifteen feet high, a bit more than twenty-five feet from the edge of the deck to the back wall. The house is all cinderblock, ruthlessly depressing cinderblock. There are no wings to speak of and no fly space. And, as one might expect, no budgets. But the very fact that we had no money made the end result even better. *Forum* turned out to be one of the best assignments of my theatrical life because we had fun with it, even with little things that we knew the audience wouldn't get—for example, the T-shirts the Proteans wore when they came out as Roman citizens accusing Pseudolus of theft. On the shirts were the giant letters S, P, Q, and R, the abbreviation for the Latin phrase "the people of Rome," except the actors came onstage with their letters out of order and had to hastily reshuffle to get them aright. I doubt ten people got that gag, but we left it in anyway because it was such a part of the overall conceptual approach: stand-up improv, where anything backstage became a prop or a costume, no matter how seemingly inappropriate, and where the visual jokes were almost as rapid-fire as the verbal ones.

Since then, we've worked on serious plays as well: *The Crucible* and *Picnic* and *Dark of the Moon*. But because Scott loves musicals (not only for their large casting opportunities but the potential financial return), it's those we tackle more often than not—and rarely are they simple little shows. Rather, it's *Guys and Dolls, The Music Man, Annie, Once on this Island, The Sound of Music, Into the Woods, Bye Bye Birdie*. It's almost frightening sometimes to open an e-mail from him because I never know what he's going to throw at me next.

I do all these for free. I say that not to boast (ooo, how generous!) but because it's the right thing to do. It gets the students interested in theatre, which is nice if we want theatre to hang around for a few more generations. Sometimes it's a ton and a half of work, with page after page of drafting revision. And yet, at the same time, the very challenge of taking a show as sprawling as *The Music Man* and making it work on their stage (and within their budget) is absolutely alluring. Over the years, we've laughed about his "look, don't shoot me, but . . ." approach to telling me what he wants to do next, and yet somehow we always manage to pull it off.

In exchange for donating my services, I get a unique laboratory, one where I can play with concept to my heart's content. It works out as an interesting relationship: he comes up with the script, I come up with the approach, and together, we make a play happen. Through that experimentation, I have learned to distill and simplify ("distill and simplify"—remember that, you're going to hear it a lot) and yet do so in a way that never lets the audience forget what show they're watching. In the process, I've discovered the importance of finding that one key piece of design that can bind the production together from start to end. No matter what play it might be, that key exists.

Bear in mind that a design key doesn't mean a unit set, although it might be one. Neither is it a color or a shape or a line or a "conceptual metaphor" or the *au courant* line in university theatre classes, the "ruling idea"—although it could be any of these as well. The key is more elusive than that. Here, it means that particular piece of the puzzle that lets you see the other 4,999 in place without having to rely on the box cover. It's reading the script and talking to the director—and then having sufficient faith in your own vision to take everything you've learned, turn it 90 degrees, and look at it afresh. It requires intuition, the ability to play "what-if" on a deeper, more visceral level. Played properly, it will tell you your conceptual metaphor, your ruling idea, and your color, shape, and line, and it will do so in one grand, sweeping gesture.

Further, bear in mind that this isn't about being so conceptually adventuresome that the audience (not to mention the producer, the cast, and the rest of the crew) sits there, looks at your work of genius, and collectively says, "Huh?" You know the kind of productions I mean: ones with overscaled imagery designed to metaphorically and visually evoke the plight of Natalie in search of her nightie. If you truly want to see design victims, you really don't have to look much farther than the classics. Somehow we got this idea that, when it comes to certain great classics of the performing arts, you shouldn't leave well enough alone, that it's not enough somehow to trust the script. We have to dress it up in clothes that don't fit. And even if they do, we have to make sure they're in the worst possible colors. Opera and Shakespeare can be a field day for the high design concept gone hopelessly wrong to the point of obliterating the story in search of a new way to tell the same damn old story. For example, a recent German production of *The Flying Dutchman* took act two's chorus of maidens and put them all on exercise bikes.

For the Spinning Song.

Get it?

Yeah, I thought it was a fairly lame joke myself. But what made it worse was that it was a one-joke visual; it wasn't tied to anything else in the production to give it context. As I tell my design students, you can set *King Lear* on Mars and make it work, but only if your approach is consistent and communicative. It has to communicate with the audience, and part of that communication comes from discovering the central key to the design.

The challenge, of course, is figuring out what the key is. Every script has one. Sometimes it requires thinking slightly outside the play's predetermined box—for example, approaching *Fiddler on the Roof* as a story told not to the audience but to the people of Anatevka on the road after their village has been destroyed. Or perhaps it's seeing *Forum* as improv comedy and then building a production where a colander and a whisk broom become a soldier's helmet. Once you have that helmet in your hand, finding out where you must go with the rest of the production can be as joyously slapstick as the musical itself.

(Sorry to interrupt again. I'm not talking about directorial concept, although certainly the key can be discovered in tandem with the director's approach to the play. In some small respect, you are playing director a bit because you'll have to anticipate how the set will work once it's installed on the stage. But whatever you're doing must supplement what your director is doing, not the other way around. Of course, if you're directing as well as designing, feel free to ignore this paragraph.)

This freewheeling approach has helped me enormously in my development as a designer in theatres far larger and better equipped than Washington County. To each I bring that search for the one piece of design that will tie the production into a neat, fiscally responsible, yet artistically satisfying package. Inspiration can come from anywhere if you leave yourself open to it. For example, for *The Shape of Things*, it was all about a statue. For *Gypsy*, a suitcase. For *Hay Fever*, the paintings of Mondrian—but not as a style source; rather, it was seeing those colorful, yet hard-lined geometrics as a way of looking holistically at the world of the play and the people who inhabit it.

Once that key is discovered, the remainder of the job is seeing how far I can go with the least number of additional elements. As I said earlier, before my career in theatre, I worked as a graphic designer and illustrator. My design mentor Tom Melnichek once told me, "Boil it down to the essentials, then throw out one more thing. But you have to be dead certain what that one more thing is before you toss it." His theory of design was that at some point you have to trust the readers to make that last, vital connection, that forcing them to do so will engage them more. And that same theory holds for theatre as well, if you think about it. If you give the audience just enough to put the pieces together, they're more involved with the play. Yes, the script says you will need a chair here and a door there, but maybe you don't really need the door. Maybe it only drives the technical director crazy and cramps the actors' style. Maybe just the chair says everything you need to say.

Or maybe it's just the door, and the chair can exit stage right, pursu-ed by bear.

Or maybe it's just the door and the chair and nothing else. No flats. No rugs or lamps or sideboards. Just a door and a chair.

It all depends on what your key is, and what it unlocks in the process.

But that right there presents a theatrical tightrope without a net. How far can you strip things down before the production starts to look underdesigned? Will the concept, when reduced to such a minimum, still speak to the audience? As with haiku, every choice has to be made carefully, and yet when it works, the result can be a thing of singular beauty.

And while squeezing a big show down to a small stage can be a challenge, sometimes an even bigger one is taking something like *The*

Fantasticks' single platform and cardboard moon and making them work on a stage fifty feet wide without losing the actors in the process. I've done it. It's hard work, but it can be done, and the same rules about finding the key still apply. You're just turning the telescope around, as it were.

And that's just on the design side. The economics of this approach should be obvious by now, but just in case they aren't, consider: if your sense of the key tells you that your play is about a particular row of columns that will be onstage throughout the entire play, then the directorial and design challenge comes to making that row of columns work. And work. And work. They're not to sit there and look pretty; they have a job to do. And in the end, if 90 percent of your resources have been put into those columns, but they're also doing 90 percent of the work, then it's money better spent than on those three large, oddly painted wagons that are onstage for eight minutes. In this regard, you're getting not only maximum design bang for your buck, but maximum economic mileage out of that buck as well. It's making sure the expense will extend as far as the concept—and a good design key will do that for you every time.

So see this as a somewhat different approach to theatre design. Yes, you still need to read the script and see where the play is set and where the actors go. It's not entirely about "gee, this feels like a . . . a . . . *red* play," although that's not entirely out of the realm of possibility. But it's looking at the play on a deeper, more visceral level and having faith in your own interpretation.

Together we're going to explore some of these. The case studies, all designed for and produced by a small high-school theatre department, range from large-scale musicals to character-driven straight plays. None of the budgets for these productions was anywhere near what you would call "high"; the median was about five hundred dollars for sets and costumes. A portfolio of other designs for other companies follows, with commentary about the conceptual process behind the work. A few of the portfolio pieces are just designs, never built save in the theatre of my own mind, yet still serve as viable examples of stripping a script down to its most succinct. Others represent first- or second-draft sketches; solutions that, in my humble opinion, worked better than the final realized design. Still others are the finished designs that appeared onstage. For those of you still determined to do it, there's a *Grease* production in there as well.

Understand this: this is not a "how-to" book about theatre design. You will find neither working drawings nor photographs. This is an idea book, one where we play with concepts and possibilities. There are no wrong solutions at this point in the design process. Everything, from the most traditional to the most absurd, is fair game, and it's my hope that you'll look at this book as "virtual permission" to explore. If it takes you into the realm where *Virginia Woolf* is performed completely in black leather and ostrich feathers, so be it. Follow that road and see where it takes you. Maybe you'll have to backtrack and (excuse the pun) restrain yourself a bit, but at least you will have gone to see what's there, and perhaps there's something useful to be found. We're not interested in the destination but the voyage, so in the main you'll see the same preliminary designs the various directors did.

As such, you'll be looking at all this from an entirely different angle than your standard design book. This is one where the understanding of the play's scenic and/or costume needs goes deeper than knowing how many stock four-by-eight platforms and boys' size 12 shirts you have. Some of this will sound like dramaturgical research; some of it will sound like agonizingly airy-fairy-oh-my-god-what-kind-of-design-is-that nonsense. But above all, it's about learning to allow yourself to take a few creative risks, without blowing your budget in the process.

(OK, one final caveat: Your design may be amazing, incredible, a delight to behold, but the minute it upstages the actors, you're dead meat. Sure, sometimes the audience wants a side order of eye candy with their serving of O'Neill, but if the wonder and majesty that is your design doesn't recede into the background within the first thirty seconds of the performance, you haven't done your job properly. Brutal, but true, folks. Remember, like I said earlier, a good set is like the host of a really swell party: he lets the guests in the door, serves them their first drink, then gets the heck out of the way. Your set should do exactly the same thing—except for the drinks thing, of course.)

In the designs presented here, I hope to demonstrate that, with proper planning and a bit (OK, more than a bit) of creativity, you can give your audience something unique, no matter how much of a tired warhorse the play itself might be. And you can do it cheap. Some of these are downright Brechtian, while others might recall the elegant shorthand of William and Jean Eckart. As visually disparate as these may seem, the thread that connects them is a love of pure theatre, a realm where, at its simplest, a single actor and a single well-chosen chair and a single light can create an entire universe. Hopefully, they will inspire you to wander off the well-beaten path of cookie-cutter *Our Town's* and find your own vision of Grover's Corners.

And if you save a few bucks in the process, so much the better, right?

A Few Design Basics

So LET'S SAY YOU'VE BEEN ASKED TO DESIGN
a set for *The Odd Couple*. You read the script and think, OK, no big
challenge here. It's a living room; how tough can that be? Yeah, Felix
is a neat freak, but that just means I have to keep it clean, right? As
long as the doors are in the right place, and you can get around the
couch without banging your shins on the coffee table, it doesn't
matter all that much, right?

Well, yes, right.

And no, wrong.

Yes, you can just slap a few flats together and put in some furniture and have a perfectly acceptable living-room set in a matter of a few
hours. But what does it say about Felix? Or about life in Manhattan on
the upper West Side? Or about letting go so you can regain control,
which is really what *The Odd Couple* is about? What would this set say
about its occupants and their world that distinguishes it from any other
play requiring a couch and a couple of chairs?

That's where it starts to get tough, so we're going to look at a few
design basics to help you maneuver through the visual minefield that
is your script, your director, your actors, and their various needs for the
production.

There are seven basic precepts of good art: order, design, tension,
composition, balance, light, and harmony. These precepts apply
whether you're talking about an oil painting or a department store display window, but they work especially hard in theatre because this is a
place where so many applications of the same precepts collide. Conceptually, they overlap, so our discussion here will look at a few of
them in the broadest of strokes and definitions.

(I'll also add that these definitions are my own interpretations and not necessarily the classic ones. Remember: the goal here is in the application, not the semantics.)

ORDER

Remember the children's song, "One of These Things Is Not Like the Others"? Sing it to yourself, a lot if need be, when considering order in your design. To create an ordered whole, everything in the design schema must connect. Out of all of these precepts, this is sometimes the toughest to follow, especially for amateur theatres whose resources are at their minimum. Still, for your design to succeed, the eye has to be able to move easily and gracefully from one thing to another, even in a design where discordance might be the goal, which suggests that, even in chaos, you need to find at least one thread that will bind the design together as a whole.

Like I said, this is one of the toughest to follow because it requires you to look at your design both in its totality and in the details at the same time. You have to watch for consistency of line in both the architecture and the furnishings. You have to consider the overall impact when making choices about those minutiae, whether props or paint. You have to remember the textures as an aggregate, so that they create the overall tactile sensations you want, whether rough hewn or polished.

For a box set, this is much like an interior design exercise and a psychological portrait at the same time. The color of the walls and the curtain fabric and the flower vases all work in concert to create a unified statement about the room, but you can't forget that you're also making a statement about the story. You want your design to speak to the tone of the play, echoing and reverberating it visually, and you do this by making design choices that complement and support it. In general, you wouldn't use bright and cheery colors and streamlined furnishings for a Lillian Hellman tragedy, nor would you use heavy, ponderous textures for a farce.

(Well, OK, actually, you might, but only if the goal was to create a schism between the set and the actors. Feydeau's highly mechanical farces, for example, work best when the chaos ensues in an environment of complete and utter control, while some of Pinter's work expressly demands white walls and simple furnishings. But notice that I say "in general.")

"That's obvious," you say to me emphatically, to which I reply, you're right. It is. But it's also one of the biggest missteps we designers make when we're working with stock pieces. We'll grab a couch because it's sorta kinda what we had in mind, even though we know the minute it appears onstage that it's completely and utterly wrong. Still, it's a couch, and whatdya want anyway?

What you want is to think like your characters. These are the people living in the world you're creating, so you have a certain obligation to give them something they would find—well, perhaps not always comfortable, but at least familiar. And this is where order will kick into gear. For example, consider Michel Tremblay's *Hosanna*, which takes place in a run-down mess of an apartment occupied by a late-middle-aged drag queen in a blue-collar neighborhood of Montreal. For all the profusion of wigs and dresses and tacky perfume bottles and mismatched furnishings, everything has been chosen by the man living there, and he made those choices with a singular vision based on his own life experience. He will prefer one shade of gold spray paint over another, just as he will prefer one kind of sequined material over another. Those preferences in texture, color, and form will reflect in everything from his drag outfits to his bath towels—and it is those preferences that will bring order into your design.

Now, yes, sometimes you have to impose order. If the couch in the storage room isn't exactly right, you have to look at it and ask yourself what it needs to make it right. No, a 50s-era couch cannot be made into a stick-style cottage one without major rebuilding, but there are other ways of changing it to get it closer to the ideal. Maybe it's a quick paint job on the visible structure. Maybe it's a fast reupholstery job or even just a simple throw. Maybe it's adding some architectural detail that will suggest the period you want to evoke. All this is possible if you allow yourself to think in terms of gestures instead of specifics. In that regard, look at what your actors do: they take their characters and sketch them for presentation. They don't live their characters' lives 24/7, just long enough for rehearsal and performance. They evoke their roles. So it can be for that couch: it needs just enough to evoke the idea.

For something more conceptual, like a musical, you initially think less as a identifiable character and more as an identifiable community. In general (and once again, "in general," because there are exceptions), in a musical you're less concerned about any one character's particular vision and more concerned about saying something holistic about the world in which that character lives. Your design order here will come from the overarching style you bring to bear, whether it's the medieval fantasia of *Camelot* or the severe Manhattan lines of *Company*.

Don't misunderstand: once you've determined that, then you have to think once again like your characters. There may be stylistic lines that visually connect the hay and feed store with the millinery shop, but Horace Vandergelder will interpret those lines differently from Irene Molloy. And if you've done your job, your audience will see a continuity from one to the other and yet also note a difference in style that separates the hard-nosed Horace from the romantic Irene.

DESIGN AND COMPOSITION
Imagine an empty stage. Just the proscenium and the back wall and the deck, nothing more.

Now put a chair somewhere on it.

Congratulations, you've just created a composition.

Composition is exactly what it says it is, the act of placing things on a stage. And where they're placed can communicate a great deal about the world in which your characters live. That chair, just by position, can either scream out its own self-importance or be shy as the proverbial wallflower. It can be confrontational or secretive—and this has nothing to do with its color or styling, just where you put it. Go back to your stage with one chair on it. Now add a second chair.

Chances are, you put it next to the first one. These two chairs now share a direct connection, and were you to put two actors in them, you would immediately be giving your audience a clue about their relationship. But now I want you to put it someplace completely different, on the other side of the stage, either up- or downstage from the first one.

Now look what it does to your composition. The mood on the stage has changed drastically—just with two chairs.

Two chairs positioned to establish connection.

Now go one step further and turn one of the chairs around so it faces upstage. Depending on which one you chose, you're either creating an atmosphere of connection or one of division.

Just with two chairs.

So why is that?

The act of recognizance. An audience will embark on a journey of discovery the moment the curtain first rises. Within those first few, vitally important seconds, they will look at your set and draw all manner of information from it, depending on what they recognize. They'll deduce who the people are that live in it, what period the play is taking place in, what time of day or season of year it is, even whether it's a comedy or a tragedy. And they do this by the visual clues you as a designer provide. One audience member might look at a set with two chairs and say to himself, "These two chairs are pointed away from each other. That tells me something about the people who'll be sitting in them later on."

Another might think, "OK, I know this one here is a nineteenth-century chair that looks a little beat up and a little worn. Chances are, the folks that own it probably don't have a lot of money and make due with hand-me-downs."

Two chairs positioned to establish distance, tension, and hostility.

Still another might think, "Hmmm, that other chair is way upstage and facing away from me. Someone's got a secret."

In all instances, your viewers are starting from the same general statement: I know what a chair is and what it's used for. From that base knowledge, they can spin off in a hundred different directions, depending on any other visual information you've given them.

There's also the fundamental geography of the stage. Regardless of its size or scale, a proscenium stage can be divided into six areas, each with its own distinct energy, as it were. Downstage center (DSC) is, of course, the most powerful: it speaks directly to the audience, all of the audience, evenly across the board. It shouldn't be at all surprising that, in a traditional living-room box set, the couch is almost invariably DSC—or as close to it as the director can get. The next most powerful positions are downstage left and downstage right: The energy in these sides is just as strong, but now it's felt by only part of the audience. The upstage sections also have variant authority: Upstage center is more powerful than upstage left and right—indeed, it's slightly more so than either downstage side. And, perhaps not so surprisingly, the power of each of these is contingent on the amount of direct connection your audience has with that particular part of the stage.

But this isn't to imply that everything but DSC is somehow weak and therefore not worth your consideration. Instead, these areas can "talk" to each other: a designer does this by creating lines that connect them, either literally (like a wall that angles from upstage center to downstage right) or visually (by having two pieces of furniture set at certain points and facing each other). These lines then shift the overall energy of the stage, for example taking some of the power of the DSC position and transferring it upstage right by using pieces that relate to each other (either by shape or, as we'll discuss next, color). This way, we can build an overall stage composition that can be extraordinarily complex by using only a few pieces to define it.

When working in a thrust or environmental situation, the areas change a bit, but not in expected ways. For example, in a thrust space, the most powerful position is, of course, the center of the stage. The next most powerful areas aren't the sides, as you might expect, but the corners because of the increased tension in the dynamic of the space. And once more, using set pieces to "talk" across the space—particularly if the lines cross center stage—can increase the design's complexity without increasing the amount of stuff onstage.

Composition is also predicated by color. Go back to your original chair on a stage and imagine it a certain color, say a wood tone, maybe a simple pine. Now change it to something completely different: if it was a pine before, make it neon orange. Now, a pastel blue. In each case, stop and consider what the color does and how it changes your feeling about everything—not just your chair, but the stage overall, the world in which that chair resides.

We're not going to get into a detailed analysis of color theory, because that's a whole book by itself. But there are a few essentials you should remember, such as the psychological and emotional impact of certain colors. Red is energy, full of fire and passion. Yellow is friendly and bright, while blue is all calmness and stability. These primary colors—red, yellow, and blue—result in the strongest, purest emotional responses. But look what happens when you start mixing them to create the secondary colors. When you mix colors, you also mix the emotional tags that accompany them. Take the friendly light of yellow and add it to the intensity of red—and you get orange, a color that evokes heat. Not a blazing, out-of-control hotness, but a consistent, steady warmth, one more inviting: a hearth, not a bonfire. That same light, friendly yellow mixed with the calmness of blue gives you green, a hue that suggests nature, vegetation, a sense of quiet happiness. From there, you can make things even more complex by creating the tertiaries: colors that result from mixing a secondary with an adjoining primary. That quietly happy green can become a content bluish green or a giggly yellow-green, depending on which way you push it and what emotion you're adding as a result.

A quick word about the problem child of the color wheel: purple. Truth be told, not many people have a clue about purple. According to Martha Stewart, who probably knows more about color than anyone outside Sherwin-Williams, a grayish shade of violet called periwinkle is the perfect color because it's the one that sets off every skin tone to its best advantage. I trust Martha on this, so there is some hope when dealing with this inordinately tricky hue.

My theory is that purple is an inherently complicated color because it mixes heated passion with cool stability, and what does that result in? Passionate stability? An intense calm? Maybe this is why we associate purple with royalty and religion: it's a mystical color that defies logic, just as we hold priests and kings in awe for no other apparent reason than the fact that we're supposed to.

Nevertheless, if a director comes to you and says, "I want this set in purple," ask whatever deity you worship for insight and wisdom. You're going to need it.

There are other ways of modifying colors and, as a result, modifying the emotional response to them. Red can be progressively lightened to pink, blue can be desaturated to shale, and all these new colors will convey additional layers of meaning to your audience. As noted in the section on order, all of them should be best considered from the point of view of the character living in his or her world: a Horace would have a hay and feed store with basic, primary colors that convey his no-nonsense view of life, while Irene's hat shop might be a study in lighter, more romantic pastels.

Ever wonder why we associate pink with girls and light blue with boys? It's because red is an emotional color, while blue isn't. Girls are taught to share their feelings, boys to hide them. Should it be surprising that we lay the groundwork for that when they're infants?

At this point, you may be thinking, "Well, this all sounds simple enough. If I want a happy set, I'll use yellow. It's like ordering from a catalogue."

Hmmm. Not quite. You see, our response to a color changes according to the other colors around it. Let's start with a bright yellow wall for that happy set of yours. It's simple, cheery, uncomplicated, exactly what you ordered. Put a blue chair in front of it, and you probably won't even notice the incremental shift in the way you perceive that yellow. But add a purple chair next to the blue one, and no doubt you'll see that wall as a cool shade of yellow. As a result, your happy set will be . . . well, yes . . . still happy, but now with a sense of seriousness, of purpose. But still happy.

Now change the blue and purple chairs to red and orange, and you'll swear the wall is a warm shade, even though the yellow itself hasn't changed. And the happiness will be taken up a notch: not quite mad delirium, but certainly more joyful than before, all because you added these passionate, warm colors. As before, what has changed is what's next to it, and these additional colors alter our perception because we throw in new pieces of visual information that influence our audience's thinking.

Or change the wall to solid black, and that orange chair fairly leaps out at you in newfound intensity. Yellow screams, as does green. But here's the curiosity: as you move away from yellow in either direction— toward red or toward violet—the difference in intensity drops off. Purple against black is little different from purple against white. What will factor the degree of intensity now is the amount of the two colors involved: a little red against a lot of black is the chromatic equivalent of a gunshot, as anyone who saw Edward Gorey's *Dracula* will attest.

Nor is it restricted to setting colors against black or white. Start with that yellow wall we used earlier. Add a few orange chairs, a table painted pumpkin, and maybe a couple of vases in shades of burnt umber and terra-cotta. Now put a blue flower in one of those vases. Rest assured that, as their eyes move around the set, the first place the audience will land on is that blue flower. Now the choice of the shade of blue becomes even more important because, with all this attention put to it, your blue flower can be everything from a drunken sorority girl to a quiet sophisticate.

But why do people notice it in the first place? They notice it because it contrasts to just about everything else on the stage. You've probably seen a color wheel: a circular representation that goes from red to orange to yellow to green to blue to violet and to red yet again. Pick any color, then look at the one directly opposite it. This is called the complementary color—orange and blue or yellow and violet. They complement each other because, were they to be placed side by side, they would bring out the most chromatic intensity of any combination possible when using either of them.

Those on either side of a particular color constitute the harmonics, the ones that work as a family of hues—red, orange, and yellow, for example, or orange, yellow, and green. Within these family sets, one color will usually predominate, but not necessarily the one in the middle.

Finally, there is the cultural baggage that comes with color. Design a room in green and red, and your audience will immediately think of Christmas. Use an overwhelming amount of white, and they'll associate it with a virginal bride on her wedding day—except for someone from China, who will sit there and weep, because white in China is the color of funerals. In addition, the lighter a color is, the more "feminine" your audience will see it; the darker, the more "masculine." (Brides wear white; grooms wear black.)

Quite a lot to think about, huh? We started with the simple act of putting a single chair on an empty stage and follow it through to the subtle complexities of a blue flower in an otherwise warm-toned room. So how do you manage something like this so the composition, whether in form or in color, doesn't slide away from you?

There are a number of ways, but the one I prefer is the three-step process. First, have something—just one thing—predominate in the design, whether by form or by color or (best of all worlds) by both. Second, surround it with the shapes, forms, and colors that otherwise support your predominant piece. Finally, for the third step, insert the little grace notes that fill in and inform the space, yet still work off that predominant piece. In your typical living-room set, for example, the couch will probably be the first step. You'll position it so it commands the full attention of the room. Then come the walls, whose positions and colors are determined by the traffic lines of the blocking, which invariably lead us back to the couch: those are your second step. The third comes in the set dressing: the pictures on the walls, the small table next to the couch, the lamps, the side chairs—all of which are chosen and placed so that, once again, they direct the eye back to that couch. Everything supports your central focus.

But just when you thought we were out of the woods . . .

BALANCE AND TENSION

While every circus act thrills and enthralls us, few beat the sheer visceral pleasure of the tightrope. High above us, a man walks across a space on nothing more than a thin cable. To do this, he has to maintain perfect balance. The slightest shift from one side to the other can cause him to fall, and we watch in an atmosphere of unrelenting tension—hoping he'll make it safely to the other side but not knowing for certain until he reaches that little platform at the end.

And so it is with our designs: Balance and tension are adjuncts to composition. But unlike that high-wire act, balance isn't just a matter of making sure you have an equal amount of "A" on either side of the

The relentless perfection of a symmetrical set.

An asymmetrical design, where all the pieces visually converge on the chair.

stage's center line. Symmetrical sets certainly have their uses and can say a great deal about the characters in the play—that they're even-handed folk, emotionally calm. Taken to an extreme, these über-balanced designs are dispassionate to the point of detached and cold. They're cerebral, not emotional, which only heightens the response we feel to characters like Oedipus or Hedda Gabler, characters who stand in sharp contrast to their perfectly ordered worlds.

But a perfectly balanced set, as noted, doesn't have to be symmetrical; there are other, more interesting ways to create that sense of poise and stability. In an asymmetrical design, you can use mass to create equilibrium: a large element on one side of the stage balanced by a smaller one or two on the other. Look at your stage as a see-saw. Two kids of even weight can play back and forth for hours, but put a heavy child on one side and a slight one on the other, and what happens? The heavier one drops to the ground and leaves the lighter one stuck in midair. There's no balance—until the heavier one moves closer to the center. At a certain point, moving that weight restores the balance.

So it is with visual balance. If you have two scenic elements, one large and one small, you can reclaim balance in your design by shifting the larger one closer to center stage while moving the smaller one further away. A single chair will balance out a twelve-by-eighteen-foot

Placed properly, a small chair can balance a big wall.

wall, if the two elements are placed so their respective masses play off each other across the center line.

Returning briefly to the previous section, we can also use color to establish balance between two disproportionate elements. A chair painted a brilliant crimson will hold its own against a wall of desaturated green—because the colors are complementary (balance across the color wheel) and the degree of brilliance and saturation has been equalized. Here, balance has been created by using the same degree of change in intensity (more for one, less for another) on both.

A good composition has perfect balance, and as you can see, good balance can be carried off with little things playing off big things. But even with balancing them out, there's still our emotional response to the potential for the big thing to overwhelm the little thing. That uncertainty results in another way to engage your audience: tension.

Creating tension is as easy as putting something on an angle. Once again, start with an empty stage and a chair. Face it: there's not much excitement in the room.

But tip it at an angle, and we're riveted because it has all this potential energy. It's not safely on the ground anymore; now it's got the possibility of falling over, and we sit there in expectation, waiting for the inevitable Law of Gravity to take over. The resulting, unrelieved

Tension created by nothing more than a chair set an an angle

tension drives us nuts because we need something to happen: either the chair will be set aright or it'll fall and hit the deck. But until it does, we can't look at anything else.

All right, assume a stagehand came out and put it back on all four feet once more. Everything reverts to a nice, uninteresting stability. Add a second chair and separate them to the far edges of the stage. While the disconnect between these two is a little more interesting, it's still just sorta, well, bland. Even a little dull on the Audience Emotional Response-O-Meter. But put those chairs in opposite corners of the stage, and tension returns because the presentation is suddenly uneven. One chair is more important than the other. Which one gets the power is dependent on how you placed them—ah-hah, you should be thinking, composition!—but the essential fact remains that by setting them on that diagonal, we give them unequal visual weight and therefore unequal importance.

Now put the upstage one on a three-foot platform. Raising one element, even in the same plane, is yet another means of creating tension, and once again, how you subsequently compose the placement of the two chairs will determine the direction of the eye's movement around the set and the audience's emotional response. Turn the higher chair to face the lower one and turn the lower one to face the audience, and they will look at the lower one because the composition, the balance, and the tension have all worked together to draw their eyes there. Turn the lower one to face the platform and turn the higher one toward the lower one, and you've created a scene of submission with two scenic "characters" facing each other but one in a position of visual superiority. Now turn the higher one to face the audience, and you've included them in your chair's plan for world domination.

Makes you want to take a little lie-down, doesn't it. Order, balance, color, tension, composition—and all you wanted to do was throw together a simple little living-room set for *The Odd Couple*. Yes, you can do that, but thinking like Felix for a few moments can push your design up a notch or two and transform it from the ordinary to The Statement. You know what color paint he would choose for the walls, what style of furniture would go where, what the view would be outside the window: everything that tells us at curtain up all we need to know about this fussy, obsessive man and his fussy, obsessive world. That way, when Oscar shows up and starts throwing dirty laundry around, the effect is all the more outrageous: he has ruthlessly violated the purity of the home, and at the same time it's hysterical to look at.

Enough theory. Let's go design a play.

CASE STUDIES

A Funny Thing Happened on the Way to the Forum

an improv set for an improv show

All right, let's start with *Forum*, since it was what got me into this in the first place.

Washington County was producing it for its entry in the regional one-act play competition in 2001. An inspired choice, *Forum* is such a cool show on many levels: silly enough for kids, rowdy enough for adults, great opportunities for actors to chow down on a few sets and for singers to do a few star turns. Scott had whittled it down to a well-paced forty-seven minutes in length, with five musical numbers that fittingly showcased his talented young performers.

For a designer, *Forum* is a field day. According to the script, the set is as straightforward as it gets:

> A street in Rome. Stage center stands the house of SENEX;
> on either side, the houses of LYCUS and ERRONIUS.

But the tone of the script almost demands you design that street in a style that matches the outrageousness of the characters. Still sounds pretty simple thus far, right? Read a little further, and you find out that Senex's house has an upper balcony, and there are second-floor windows on the other two. Costume-wise, it's equally simple; with only a few exceptions, everyone gets one costume. The Proteans—a chorus of three in the original production, four in ours—change a few accessories to suggest a wider range of characters: sailors, soldiers, Roman citizens, and so on. Cut through it all, and *Forum* is one of those shows everyone loves to do because it's almost foolproof. It's a wonderful script attached to a brilliant score built around a bunch of slapstick vaudeville characters. Bottom line: you have to screw up pretty mightily not to make *Forum* work.

However . . .

(You knew it was coming, right?)

The problem came when I had to factor in that the set had to travel to competition and that the kids themselves had to set it up and that they only got a certain amount of time in which to do so before they had to perform. The rules for state one-act competitions are pretty ruthless when it comes to time; if you're not done in fifty-five minutes, the judges start deducting points. And in some competitions, that fifty-five-minute limit has to include everything: set up, performance, and tear down to make way for the next school.

Suddenly, this easy show got a little more problematic. Suddenly, I had to consider that it and the props and the costumes were being carried around in something about the size of a small rental van, and it all had to fit, while at the same time look comfortable on a stage thirty feet wide. Suddenly, this simple little riff on a Roman comedy started to look like a logistical nightmare. Three two-story units that collapse down to fit in an SUV? Possible, but they'd have to be in so many pieces that I might as well provide Washington County with a jigsaw puzzle. At the same time, if I wanted the walls in a single piece, I'd need ten-foot flats at the very least, and I couldn't see any way of those arriving to the competition intact with the van's rear door open for the entire trip. Then there are the step units, which would eat up even more precious storage space.

So what to do? The clue came early in act one when Pseudolus is checking that he has all the ingredients needed for a sleeping potion, among them, horse sweat. "Where am I going to find mare's sweat on a balmy day like this?" he moans.

And yet, not one page later: "Would you believe it? There was a mare sweating not two streets from here." It's a wonderfully sly little moment, a wink at the audience that says, "Yeah, we know it's absurd, but we're going to slide right over it even though it makes no logical sense whatsoever." *Forum*, of course, is full of such things: the whole plot of the play is contingent upon one coincidence building on another of the most outrageous sort, but this is the first really bald example, almost to prepare the audience for the nonstop nonsense that follows. Reading that line and knowing how it was supposed to work,

I suddenly knew what the basics of the set needed to be. I was still missing the key that would define everything, but I was on my way.

The detail about the mare's sweat is pivotal because it says, deftly and elegantly (and hysterically), that this is a scripted comedy meant to sound like an improvisation. No need to explain anything about how Pseudolus got it or any deal he had to negotiate with the owner of said mare or even how the horse might have felt about it. Pseudolus needs sweat; he goes offstage, and he comes back with sweat. It's that simple. And the play moves on. Later, when things are flying completely out of control, a few gaggles of geese are all that are needed to resolve the hopelessly convoluted plot. And we just accept it. Not because it necessarily works, but specifically because it doesn't have to.

By now, you might have some idea where all this is leading, but let's play a bit more. Improv comedy is a long-standing tradition in the theatre. It's possible the earliest Attic comedies were little more than topical skits with music and dancing, but improvisation really took off in the Middle Ages with commedia players. Transient actors, they moved from town to town, set up a temporary stage, and performed in front of crudely painted drop curtains. They had no scripts per se, just broad outlines of plots and stock characters that were so stylized and defined that the audience knew instinctively who was the old man and who was the fair young maiden and who was the addle-headed doctor and the braggart soldier and so on and so forth.

Much like *Forum*, if you think about it: old man, fair maiden, braggart soldier, wily slave. These aren't characters with a lot of depth. They're all quickly sketched so we can identify their archetypes with speed and efficiency. As such, if we're to be true to the spirit of the play, the world in which these characters operate has to be equally recognizable, one where we can look at it and say, "Ah-hah!" from the moment the curtain rises (or, as it would have in Roman times, falls). If you look at virtually any production of *Forum*, the designers do pretty much that: it's not realistic Roman architecture by any stretch but more of a fantasia on it. Columns. Flutings. Tile roofs. And then, to sell the fact that it's a musical comedy, lots of color.

(Yet another little interruption. That, by the way, isn't so far from the way the Romans themselves treated their buildings. Unlike the white marble we see in most Hollywood spectacles, Greek and Roman architecture was colorful to the point of garish. The painted ladies of the Victorian era didn't hold a candle to the way these guys gussied up every little newel and every little post. And not soft little pastels: they used bright, vivid, pure tones of intense red and piercing yellow and brilliant blue. To us, Athens and Rome would probably look more like theme parks than centers of civilization.)

So let's put all this together. Three houses, with suggestions of upper levels. A script that says "Let's have a whale of a lot of fun and not worry about logic." A set that, like its commedia predecessors, has to travel. But where's the key that holds all this together? The answer lay with the play's origin, the comedies of Plautus. Not the plays themselves, you understand, but particular visual aspects of the world in which they were written.

All right, let's backtrack here. I'm a bit of a history nut, with a real love for ancient times: Greece, Rome, Egypt, Sumer, Crete, all that stuff. In my research on those times, I found that the earliest theatres were not majestic marble horseshoes but rather painted drops on a crudely built platform, much like commedia stages (ah-hah! you should be thinking by now.). The big theatres grew out of these humble origins, but if you look at both the first platforms and, for example, the Theatre at Epidaurus, you can see immediate similarities. The audience sat in a circular arrangement, and the play was mounted on one side, with an open space in the middle for dancing and an altar to Dionysus.

If you think about it for a moment, this is just the next step from early cavemen sitting around the fire at the end of the day. One of them tells a story of the hunt, using the fire as stage lights and a conveniently placed rock as scenery and the skin of the hunted animal as costume. You worked with whatever was available. We don't need to go back quite that far, of course, but knowing how early Greek and Roman plays took that conceit and developed it might be useful. Most of Roman theatre and stagecraft was lifted whole cloth from its Greek ancestor. But for all we do know about Greek theatre, there's also a lot we don't—some stagecraft mechanics and the masks, of course, but it's pretty limited when it comes to specifics. They used painted backgrounds of some kind, but we don't know what they looked like. The crane that lifts Medea is still a mystery, and we have no real examples of the *periaktoi* or the *ekkyklema*, just what's written about them in contemporary texts.

What we know about them in the visual sense is taken mostly from wall murals, mosaics, and urns. Ever seen pictures of Greek vase artwork? Everything is very stylized and very linear. Perspective takes a flying leap because that's the way the art form works. There's also this little detail that most vase painters added of captioning, adding names to characters, mostly, so you'd know this one is Heracles and that one is Ulysses. Figures on these vases were so stylized as to be interchangeable, so captioning was needed to tell one from another. That becomes useful later; for now, let's go back to that thing about perspective.

Perspective as portrayed on Greek vases was a bit of crapshoot all around. Say you have an image of a man talking to another man who happens to be inside a second-story window. On most vases, the guy on the second floor is no higher off the ground than the guy in the street if you look at this image literally. But you accept the convention that he's above because of the way the building is drawn. It's perfectly normal within the culture in which it was painted, even though it looks, to our more practiced eyes, a little goofy and strange.

That's all well and good, you say, but back to the play. Where does this lead?

Well, consider: we needed a second story on our houses, but we had no real way of building it, let alone transporting it, until I looked again at those vase paintings and realized the answer was staring me in the face. There's the key. It's not so much the visual style as the way we interpret it. Remember, to the Greeks and Romans, such imagery was perfectly normal. To us, it's something else altogether, even though we can recognize that this is a house and this is a man inside the house talking to another man outside the house. The pieces are all there, but they don't fit quite like we expect them to. We have to work a little to figure out the visual language, so we become a little more involved in the process of translation. If I used this as the lynchpin for the design, the world of the play could now become a little more unpredictable, as well as one that involved the audience.

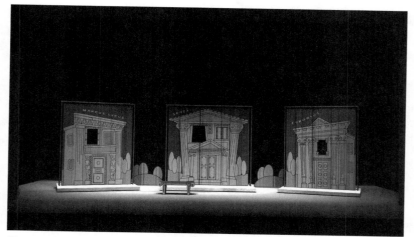

The set for Forum: *three platforms, two trampolines, and a bench*

So instead of three literal structures, we built three small platforms with painted drops. Each drop suggested a two-story structure, with windows that were (conveniently) the height of a standing actor. Cut a hole in the window, put an actor behind it, and suddenly he's on the second floor of the House of Lycus. Now the set was just as much a character of the play as Miles Gloriosus because when that actor stuck his head out that second-floor window, the set informed the audience that it intended to be as much demented, improvisational fun as the show itself.

And of course, there's the added beauty that this was easy to transport and easy to assemble, not to mention very easy on the budget. Three three-by-six platforms. Three pieces of canvas. Some PVC for the canvas to hang from. Add some hardware and a bench with a cartoony false front, and you're done. This once-problematic play became easy again, with a simplicity that worked with the script in ways that a fully constructed series of two-story houses simply couldn't begin to match.

But there's one more detail to be snatched from history and applied here. Remember the custom of captioning names to characters on those vases? Here, I took that same concept and applied it by captioning the names of the houses to the drops, giving them that little touch of ancient times that subtly underscored the musical's theatrical and historical roots.

So let's review: I started with the locale as indicated in the script, then simplified, simplified, simplified—but not in ways that reduced everything to skeletal constructs and platforming with stairs. Instead, I looked at the overall tone of the script and examined the theatre forms and cultures that made this romp possible. Using a combination of two disparate art forms, I created a set that gave *Forum* a slightly more engaging look and a slightly more edgy feel.

Next, we turned our attention to the costumes to see if we could capture that same sense of fun with the specific characters. *Forum*'s characters, as noted earlier, are all archetypes, which allow the audience to easily essay who someone is when he or she comes onstage. The pace of the script is such that quick identification is critical if the audience is going to keep up with the complexities of the plot. Someone like Erroneous has a big scene in act one, then appears only briefly throughout the rest of the play until the end, but the audience has to know immediately that this is Erroneous if they're to stay on top of things.

Greek and Roman costume is pretty straightforward: a tunic on the men, shapeless dresses on the women. (There's also the "merchandise" from the House of Lycus, but I'll discuss that in a moment.) Most of *Forum*'s basic costumes come from a little out-of-print handbook, *Greek and Roman Costume for the Theatre*. In it, the author goes into remarkable detail about color and fabric and styling, things that distinguish slaves from slave owners and Roman from Persian. If one were to do a historically accurate production of this play, this book would be a gold mine, but my interest lay in only the basic elements, just the shapes and lines, coupled with a few cultural details.

The reason, of course, is simplicity of execution. If you know all the men's costumes are taken from the same basic tunic, it's easy to whip these out. But what to do to give each character his or her individual style? For example, how do we distinguish the two old men, Senex and Erroneous, from each other?

(Some of what follows will sound like basic costume theory, so if you want to skip over it, go ahead; I won't be offended, I promise.)

The goal here, as noted, was to play off the ideas we had presented in the scenic design: the sense of improv, the feeling of audience involvement. When it comes to the two old men, Erroneous and Senex, we only needed to know that the first has been traveling the world in search of his lost children while the second is a stay-at-home retired gentleman with a bit of a lecherous streak. Let's take the letch first.

Senex, whose costume is built in layers of variated gray flannel.

There are certain things that immediately identify the little old men of the world, and first and foremost is that their clothing is a generation or two out of date. They wear the same clothes they had when they were working adults, so if we were to costume a little old man today, he'd probably be in some 50s-to-60s-era plaid, like a houndstooth jacket. To underscore his age, the clothing would be faded and grayed back to the point of being almost monochromatic. We applied that fashion sense to Senex by giving him a gray base and a simple overlay of another gray-based plaid. Immediately, his costume said little old man and Roman all at once, and it did so with a bit of comic flair as it used recognizable details and repackaged them to conform with the supposed world of the play.

For Erroneous, who has been traveling a bit, we made his tunic from camouflage-print material, since traditional camo carries a wealth of visual baggage: exotic ports of call, faraway places, someplace not here but there. We added a cloak of rough burlap (which is nothing more than a piece of material tied at the throat) and a hat made from an inverted wicker basket and presented a simple, effective portrait of a man who had spent his life on the road.

Now note: both these worked from the same basic tunic pattern. The material and a few accessory details is what distinguishes them, and so it was with the other male characters (even though our Pseudolus was actually played by a female, with no pretensions of being a man). They all looked wildly different, but the basic construction was

Proteans

The Proteans' basic costume.

based on the same essential pieces. By using painted borders (which are themselves character identifiers) and different materials and slightly different accessories, we set up sufficient visual clues for the audience to know immediately who was who.

The Proteans had a slightly different basic costume, one that looked a little more haphazard, a little less finished. Since the Proteans had to play so many alternate roles, they were the perfect place to push the idea of "improvisational costume," as though they all ran offstage, found a few pieces of stuff, and then slapped them on before returning to their performance. (Remember what I said about cavemen?) The soldier costume came first, with its trash-can-lid armor and helmets made from metal colanders and whisk brooms. The aforementioned S, P, Q, and R T-shirts quickly followed for the Roman citizen costume (an early version had the Roman citizens inside a single, gigantic T-shirt, but that was scuttled when it seemed like it might be too awkward). One of my favorite bits in the blocking came when the citizens roared onstage, Pseudolus in hand, and then realized their letters were out of order. They hastily set themselves in proper order, and the play continued.

(One thing about these add-ons that made them successful is that they were, for lack of a better word, "honest" with the audience. A metal trash-can lid was presented exactly as it is, nothing more, nothing less. Had we taken a plastic container lid and covered it with tin foil, that would have made it "dishonest" in the sense that we would have been disguising it into something it's not. These silly props all have that feeling of just plucked from backstage and thrown on—not covered or painted or "cheated." Yes, there is a lot of disguise going on in *Forum*, but sometimes what better way to hide than in plain sight?)

Miles Gloriosus had arguably the most traditional costume in the production, with his paneled overskirt and leathery suggestions of armor on top of the basic tunic. But even he had those little details that define his character: his headband with the three-star-general jewelry, the bank of military ribbons, and the way the panels on the overskirt were staggered in length so as to slyly suggest certain things about his anatomy. He's a sexual powerhouse in gold and black leather, so much so that you can't help but giggle at his "overcompensating" sense of military style.

Next were the women. We wanted the audience to know that Philia and Hero would be together by play's end, so we did a female version of his outfit: same virginal white material, same overlay, same painted border. Easy.

Ah, but Domina. Now we had some serious fun. Domina is all about presence and appearances, so the larger-than-life we could make her, the happier she'll be. True, everyone in this show is larger than life, but Domina pushes it to an extreme: she's an even larger version of the über-style-conscious housewife in *Keeping Up Appearances*. At the same time, it felt necessary to give her a costume that was, in some respects, more trouble than it was worth: perhaps awkward to wear, forcing her into odd positions—almost as if she were spending the entire evening on a fashion show runway. I wasn't exactly sure how to convey that, until I came across my handbook's drawing of a woman wearing a peplos. In essence, it's a large rectangle folded in half and then draped across the arms with a hole cut for the neck. It's about as simple as these costumes get, but it's also the one that's the hardest to wear: To keep it from dragging on the ground, Domina had to spend most of the play with her arms up, so she has this perpetual "look at me, I'm floating!" stance.

Domina: a headdress of silver pipe cleaners and a necklace of blank CDs.

You'd think that would be confining, but watching it in performance, it proved to be a bang-on perfect approach to the character. She had to back off, emotionally and physically, to maintain control. Once she changed into her copy of Philia's costume, it was almost as if the gloves had come off, and the real Domina could safely emerge: rougher, angrier, far more determined to do what was needed to keep her man—a wife you just don't mess with, period.

As with Pseudolus, Lycus was played by a female student (we do a lot of cross-gender casting, as I'm sure many high schools do), portraying the character, like Pseudolus, as a woman. I wanted to do something that would establish her as the mercenary outsider. Marcus Lycus isn't part of the regular crowd in this play: she's a used-car dealer, an oily insurance agent, a low-level sales executive. She has to stand in contrast to everyone else because she's so wonderfully unlikable. So who was unlikable in Roman times? Back to the book, where I found clothing styles from Persia. Persia and Rome spent a lot of time at each other's throats, almost as much as Persia and Greece, so positioning her as not only a foreigner, but also a suspicious foreigner, seemed a natural, especially in tandem with her profession as "procurer." When it came to her border treatment, it was a moment of inspired lunacy when I imagined credit cards lining the piece.

Lycus truly encapsulates the design approach to *Forum*'s costumes: it was almost stream-of-consciousness, where instinct took over from historical research and character development. It's a little ancient times and a little modern day, all at the same time, and it's the commentary-esque details that make the costume fun and approachable: she's a walking MasterCard, from color break-

Marcus Lycus. Note the credit-card motif.

down to stylized logo. All the costumes in *Forum* were designed quickly, but Lycus's emerged at frightening speed because everything about it—the foreign influences, the patina of commerce—just seemed right.

When we did the show the first time, the courtesans were all put in similar costumes: matching short dresses in bright neon colors. But for the revival a few years later, Scott and I thought it might be fun to individualize them. In the spirit of the Proteans' "instant costumes," they became vaudeville showgirls with distinct personalities. Collectively, they were walking Catskills jokes, some stereotypical, some subtly visual. The Geminaes' off-the-shoulder cornicing, for example, only makes sense when they're placed side by side. And for Panacea, given her name, what could be better than a Hello Nurse? They were sexy without being salacious, a difficult line to walk for a high-school production. But the combination of modern-day styling on top of ancient Rome garments underscored yet again our anachronistic, thematically freewheeling approach to the material.

Gymnasia was a bit of a creative issue. In the script, Pseudolus needs to look at Lycus's merchandise ostensibly as an "indulgence." Because Pseudolus was played by a girl, it was difficult enough to get around that particular plot point without suggesting some pretty blatant lesbianism. As such, it would seem to make sense that, with her getting Gymnasia at the end, that particular piece of merchandise should be a boy. So I designed accordingly: tanned beefcake in gold lame spandex and a wholly ornamental capelet. But with no one available to play that part in that particular way, it was back to the drawing board. Any references in the script to Pseudolus "winning" her were cut, and we slid ever so casually over the "indulgence" reference. In the second draft, she became every high-school sport ever played, all at the same time:

— GYMNASIA —

Gymnasia.

football shoulder pads, baseball socks, track and field sweatbands, even a cheerleader skirt. This bizarre combination resulted in an ensemble that got one of the night's bigger laughs when that character came onstage for the first time.

One final note about all the costumes. If you look at the costume sketches, you'll see boots on most of the characters. But we opted instead for tennis and running shoes, and that, like so many other decisions about this show, turned out to be an inspired choice. Not only did it keep costs down some more, but it also provided one more visual detail in line with the production's overarching sense of slapdash, grab-anything-that-will-work silliness.

Looking at the design holistically, it becomes readily apparent that neither the set nor the costumes is all that challenging from a construction or fiscal point of view. You're going to find that's true of all the case studies: Washington County doesn't spend a lot of money because it doesn't have a lot of money. And yet the designs all do their job and do it well because it's the little things, the details and the styling, that make them work. In turn, those details work hard: expressing character and attitude, giving each production the most bang for its scenic and couture buck. It's reducing *Forum* and *Picnic* and *Guys and Dolls* to a smaller scale, but with distillation more than simple reduction. And that, in many respects, makes these designs truer to the spirit of the play.

Picnic

Inge on the coast

Sometimes you have to turn away from the expected design because (1) you can't afford it (which was a perpetual problem at Washington County High) or (2) you don't have the manpower or time to build it (which was also a perpetual problem at Washington County High). But sometimes you have to turn away from the expected design because (3) there's something else that just plays better with the home team. In *Picnic*, it was all three.

There was the usual issue of money, but even if the money were available, the play, which takes place in Kansas, required a fairly large set: a shared backyard between a pair of two-story midwestern cottage-style houses. Scott certainly didn't have the resources in his technical theatre class to pull that off, let alone the time: We had just finished work on the one-act competition musical for that year, and there were only a scant few weeks between that production and this one. All this suggested that we couldn't follow the play exactly as scripted.

And there was, for me, a third factor: Washington County High is in Sandersville, Georgia, where Florida and the ocean aren't that far away. Folks live by the water as much as possible, and everyone has a boat and an entire wardrobe of beachwear. I had this weird idea that if *Picnic* were set on the beach and not in Kansas, the audience would identify better with the world of the play, making it an easier sell.

That, of course, left the Big Question: Would *Picnic* transplant to the coast?

OK, let's look at the Big Picture in anticipation of the Big Question. *Picnic* takes place over the Labor Day weekend. A girl "intended," as they used to say, for a rich if boring local boy suddenly falls into the arms (and everything else, for that matter) of a James Dean drifter.

There's a lot of talk about the heat. And fireworks. And just about every other 1950s euphemism for sex you can imagine.

But even though the script says it's taking place in Kansas, there's nothing specific in the dialogue to support that. For all we know based on the actual lines, this could be in Pacific Northwest or Orange County or New England. It says Kansas because almost all of Inge's major works take place in Kansas, and certainly the author's intentions should be respected. But if the theme of young lust is that universal, does it really matter where it's set?

Certainly, what the author's wants should be taken into consideration and respected. *The Madwoman of Chaillot*, for example, takes place in Paris, and it'd be difficult, if not impossible, to legitimately move it anywhere else. The attitudes and philosophies in Giraudoux's play are distinctly Parisian, so much so that setting the play in New York, for example, would require not only an extensive rewrite but also a philosophical shift. Yes, it could be done. Yes, it would be the same story of a crazy old lady who saves the world. But it wouldn't be *The Madwoman of Chaillot*. It would be *The Madwoman of Tribeca*. And it would be a profoundly different play.

At the same time, should the specific needs of the author be cast in concrete? We've seen remarkable productions of *Rigoletto* set in New York's Lower East Side and *Taming of the Shrew* as a Wild West spectacular—imaginative reworkings that succeeded in transplanting Verdi and Shakespeare to the New World without violating the ideas behind either work. So when is something like this fair game?

It comes back, once again, to consistency of concept and vision. If I am to take the liberty of moving Inge's backyard to the south Atlantic coast, I have to make sure it works unfailingly. Yes, this is playing director to a degree, so I had to pitch the idea to the real director and see if there was anything he could pick up on. This was still early in my working relationship with Scott, so his initial reaction was a cautious "um . . . OK." He agreed with the motivation for it; now it was up to me to find out if the visual presentation would violate anything in the script.

My first step was to read the dialogue and ignore the stage directions. Was there anything in the sound of the play that said it had to remain in Kansas? A few odds and ends, but bearing in mind that Inge saw only the Midwest as the "real" America, I felt safe to proceed. He was born in Independence, Missouri, and his best-known plays tell the stories of the midwestern folks he no doubt grew up with. But does that limit *Picnic* to a specific geographic locale? After all, we all want to believe that our corner of the United States is the "real" America, whether it's Topeka or San Francisco or Dallas or Ogunquit. We all want to believe that we represent the American ideal just as much as anyone else. On that point, moving the locale would actually underline the play's inherent universality.

From there, it was the specifics of the story: summer love (or lust), making mistakes as we come of age, life in a small town where anyone and anything is cannon fodder for the local gossips. The eternal conflict between the glamorous lights of the big city and the social security that comes in knowing all your neighbors. Once again, this would play anywhere, so I checked that off the list. Would it require any reimagining of the characters? Not really. The socially alienated drifter and the "woman with a past" are not unique to the Midwest.

Another factor that permitted Florida all the more is the time of year: the end of summer, the beginning of fall. There's much talk about returning to school and resuming a life of responsibility and focus. That's something that an affair with a drifter, no matter how hot he might be, just can't beat. Georgia and Florida, like southern California, live in an almost perpetual summer, free of any responsibility beyond what number sunblock to wear. Having to turn your back on that and leave the beach for school has to be one of the toughest things about being a teenager. Yes, I decided, this would work.

(Now, please note: this is not about finding justifications for your conceptual decisions. If you feel you have to justify something, then it's probably not the right choice. If anything, this is when you should be almost ruthless in your assessment and prepared to abandon it at the first sign of a textural or thematic problem.)

I still had the same scenic requirements: two houses, a fence with a gate, and a backyard. I figured the houses themselves were prefabs, maybe a step or two above trailers, based on a sense that if these were typical beach folk, they probably spent far more time outside than in.

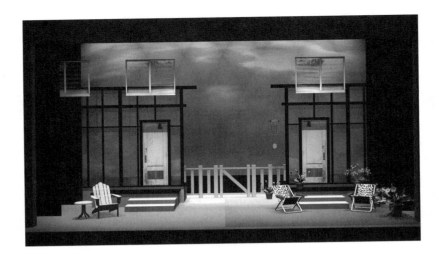

But the prefabs are about a decade old now and showing their age: the metal doors are starting to rust from the salt air, and the blinds on the second-floor windows are warped and twisted from too much direct sun. The houses themselves are scrim work, suggestive of open-glass patios on one level and, on another, a place where secrets are impossible to keep. There was something about being able to see into the houses, about being to watch private lives only moments before they become public ones that heightened the mood of the play. And behind them, an oceanfront sky in a perpetual sunset of pink and blue, courtesy of a combination of gobos and glass-slide projections. Controlling the lights on the backdrop allowed us to suggest different times of day, from midafternoon to late at night to the morning after. Finally, to counterbalance that, the deck was divided down the middle and painted the same pink and blue.

Why? It felt right.

And it looked damn cool.

And sometimes that's reason enough.

Even though this is a shared yard, the two neighbors are very different people: Madge and her family have only recently arrived, while Mrs. Potts has been around for a while. As such, her side of the yard would look more lived in, with hanging plants and flowering shrubs and a wind chime. Sexually, she's a very frustrated woman, thanks in no small part to her omnipresent mother, so I decided to alleviate that frustration a bit by giving her a set of lawn chairs upholstered in leopard skin. If she couldn't have a man, she'd at least live like she could.

We pushed the costumes to the early 60s, a time when sexual frustration was still around but teenagers might be somewhat more inclined to follow their instincts about it. It also gave the town a deceptively "pretty" look of pastels, which ran decidedly counter to the not-so-pretty atmosphere.

Everything taken in consideration, it was a painless transplant. It required no pruning of the script or the sensibilities of the characters, even as it took root and blossomed under our pink and blue sky. We maintained that integrity while also giving the audience something they could easily identify as "home turf." And, as you know, once you give them that, you draw them in a little more readily.

Would it work elsewhere? Could you pack up this play and move it to the Texas Panhandle or the California coast or even the Canadian prairies? I don't see any reason why not: this is a play whose story is not unique to the Midwest. No matter where you are geographically, you will find young people feeling trapped and drifters acting sullen and summers coming to an end. If the themes are that universal, your production should feel right at home, no matter where home might be.

Fiddler on the Roof

stories around a campfire

In *Fiddler*, the design approach takes the story and turns it around on itself, entirely for the audience's benefit. The reason for that is simple: because this musical is so well known, the audience walks into the theatre knowing full well what will happen. There's no real element of surprise. OK, granted, with every popular musical, there's zero element of surprise: we know Dolly will marry Horace, that Curley and Laurie will ride off in that surrey with the fringe on top, and that the mangiest cat of the lot makes it to Heaven. But it becomes sadder somehow with *Fiddler*. After all, this isn't a musical comedy; it's a Greek tragedy with music.

This bothered me because the gradual disintegration of that village is one of the things that makes this musical so sympathetic and embraceable; like Job, Tevye has to endure trial after trial, and even at the end, we don't know if his family survives. Did he ever see his cousin in America? Did the daughter and her husband ever escape Siberia? We can only hope they did, because the script is adamantly silent on those issues.

Still, despite that, it was the sheer popularity of this show that killed any possibility that we, as an audience, would care. The songs have become such standards that, in performance, you can't hear them in context any more. You sit there, patiently tolerating the book scenes so you can get to the next hey-I-know-that song. Autonomous beings, they have been wrenched loose through their own familiarity and now stand in agonizingly sharp relief to the script. Instead of hearing "Sunrise, Sunset" as a poignant celebration of family, you can't help but automatically slip into "oh, yeah, they sang this at Cousin Sophie's wedding." And then you catch yourself singing too, and as a result you miss everything happening to the characters onstage. You miss the reason for the song itself. And through that, you miss the reason for the play.

And I was determined not to let that happen here.

After a false start with a design that was simply too massive for the weight of this show, the key to *Fiddler* came surprisingly quickly, right on the title page itself: "Based on stories by Sholom Aleichem."

Stories.

I knew *Fiddler* was taken from a dozen or so stories about a milkman and his daughters, but it still left me thinking. OK, why do we tell stories? For a variety of reasons: to pass the time, to teach a lesson, to gain an insight, to share an experience.

All right, to share an experience: that sounds good. Where do we tell stories? Around the office watercooler. At dinner with friends. Most traditionally, at night around the campfire. Watercoolers and friendly dinners were certainly out of the question as design motivations for a serious musical about Russian Jews—but a campfire? That sounded interesting. But if we're presenting the story of *Fiddler* as something told late at night around a campfire, whom is it being told to? And why these particular stories to these particular people?

In a moment of shock and surprise, I knew: the people around this conceptual campfire were the villagers of Anatevka, the very same villagers who, in the play, will be thrown out of their homes and forced onto the road for destinations unknown. I didn't know how I knew this, but I did. Now they were refugees, taking whatever they could on carts, on horseback, on their own backs for that matter. "Why" was still open for investigation, but somehow I knew that we were seeing the end of the play right at the beginning: we just hadn't told the audience that yet.

More than the design key, that was going to be our little surprise.

(If any production for Washington County had me playing director long before Scott got his hands on the design, it was this one. This is the kind of concept that, rightfully, should have come from him, but in this case, it was the other way around, with an insistence that gave him little choice. The production pretty much came to him whole cloth, with a detailed analysis of how it was going to work onstage, how the characters would transform from anonymous refugees to the ones we know with such familiarity, even how the Russian soldiers would slide in and out of the real-time story. As a general rule, I never try to impose this much. Really, I don't, honest. Ask Scott; he'll tell you, I swear. It was just that, in this particular case, the concept was simply too good, too ripe with possibility, to ignore. Thank God he decided it was worth pursuing. Had he not, I have no idea what I would have come up with next: I was seriously married to this idea because I knew it would work.)

With the core concept in place, the foundation of the design slammed together with surprising speed. No overture (I don't even know if there is one in the score). Rather, we start with refugees, on the road after their homes had been destroyed, still "escorted" by Russian guards. Stopping for the night, they're exhausted from a long day's forced march. Our set would be a roadside, with a fence and a bower of trees. Denuded of leaves, they provide no protection from the elements, only the illusion of safety. Bearing what few things they could, the refugees huddle around a campfire. Somewhere, in this mass of frightened, hungry people, someone takes out a violin and starts to play, and someone else, sitting near the fire, starts to speak: "A fiddler on a roof . . ." There is a soft sigh of recognition, and our play begins: an entertainment not just for the audience but for the refugees as well. Suddenly, "Tradition" wasn't just a song that gives opening exposition; now it also provides reassurance and a much-needed sense of belonging and self.

As our storyteller moves into the role of Tevye, the refugees allow themselves to be caught up in the moment, taking their parts as well—the wife, the daughters, the matchmaker, the butcher. They slip into their roles as quickly as the few props around them transform into an entire village. And as these bits and pieces come together among the people, the roadside itself takes part, with the trees transforming into giant candles for the Sabbath prayer. Even the guards, watching from the sidelines, enter the story . . . but in unexpected ways that blur the line between reality and fantasy.

One major advantage was that we were performing the so-called junior version of the script, a specially edited presentation that runs in a single act for about ninety minutes. This compression from the orig-

The basic set: All furnishings were brought on at the top of act one and manipulated into place to form the various scenes.

inal play allowed us to move everything on a visually sustained pace, something we simply could not have done were we doing the full musical.

Another progression was making itself apparent as well: our refugees have stopped for the day, right around late sunset. As the play unfolds, we go deeper and deeper into the night. The lighting becomes more and more fantastical and dreamlike, culminating in multicolored projections that fill the sky for the wedding scene. Then, after the Russian "demonstration," things become more ominous and shadowy, the village's dark night of the soul, when it has to look back and remember before it can move on into the uncertain day. And as the characters within the story prepare to leave Anatevka, the refugees outside it prepare to greet the sunrise.

With the essential design determined, now it was time to knuckle down and explore specific logistics. What did we need that would say Tevye's house? No more than a table, with maybe a couple of chairs. Other houses could be conveyed by benches or crates or any place where the family could gather as a unit. Every piece we used had to come from someone in the company carrying it in at the top of the show: that was the rule. In the process, little discoveries manifested

Tevye's Dream. The benches are turned on end to become "tomb-stones."

themselves: the wedding gifts, for example, came from the refugees' most cherished possessions, the most valuable things saved before the pogrom. Through this, a simple lace tablecloth became a statement of community. Other treasures emerged from suitcases and boxes to participate in this shared experience of love and joy.

For Tevye's Dream, taking benches and turning them upright into makeshift tombstones created the graveyard. Tevye's bed was suggested by two chairs set side by side, and Grandma Tzeitel would appear from inside one of the larger crates set just upstage from the "bed." Just as our storyteller Tevye improvises on the spot, so do the refugees.

But it was in the second act when we would let the audience in on our secret. Tevye takes his daughter to the train platform, and as with every other scene thus far, benches and chairs and suitcases and trunks are arranged in a pile to suggest it. But as a final touch, someone comes forward with a singed wooden train station sign and places it, almost reverently, on top: Anatevka. At that moment, we completely draw in the audience. Suddenly, these were no longer anonymous travelers: this was Tevye and this was Motel and this was Chava. And this was what remained of Anatevka, in all its heartbreaking sadness.

Not everything I proposed made it onstage. Tevye's Dream, for example, is cut in the junior version, which I consider a shame: it's a full-cast production number in a show that doesn't have very many opportunities for the chorus. There were other things that we just never could work out technically, like the projections for the wedding scene. Still, the final production was a good chunk of the concept, and I was happy with that.

Two years after this production, I saw the Broadway revival, which set the play among birch trees and hanging lanterns. It was a lovely, delicate production, and while I seriously doubt the production team looked to a little high school in Georgia for inspiration, there were enough sympathetic echoes to tell me we had been right to follow this path.

The Crucible

drowning in religious fervor

Arthur Miller's famous take on the McCarthy era is one of those classic "historical" plays that, every now and then, needs a good dusting. This isn't just an "important" play. This is an *important* play, the kind of clarion call we need in these times of diminishing liberties. As they did when the play was first produced in the 1950s, the themes still resonate (perhaps even more so now) with their look at religious and political paranoia run wild. It's chaos in a very controlled world, one where the political leaders are, more likely than not, quick to use any ill-founded hysteria they can for personal and professional leverage.

Although timeliness was one of the main reasons for choosing *The Crucible*, a second was purely pragmatic: budget. The department was out of money for the year, and Scott's solution was to do this as a modern-dress version, which would, of course, simplify costs while also heightening the immediacy. Hmmm. A play about Puritans, but set in the modern day. That, naturally, set me spinning off into "what if" territory. What if the Puritans had remained the dominant moral and political force in the United States? And if we were to explore just a bit into this alternate history, what would we find that might relate back to Miller's play?

(Self-interruption again—but this one's important. Remember how I talked about concept in the first chapter and how dangerous it is to impose one on a work? This production veers really close to the edge, but I want you to notice how it never crosses that line. Everything we did, every decision we made, was taken from themes and ideas in the play itself. Nothing was thrown in for the sake of theatrical effect. That's important when you're examining these high-concept shows, whether the ones in this book or the ones you actually see in a theatre. You have to ask yourself: Is the work of the director and designer consistent with the play's message? Is it amplifying the ideas and the author's intent? Or is it being novel for its own sake? That's a tough question sometimes because high concept demands more of the viewer if it's to be completely understood. The concept might be buried so deeply that the production team will say, "Of course it's consistent!" without realizing that the audience wasn't in on the preproduction meetings when the elusively arcane was shoved downstage center. When that happens, it's time to step back from the tree trunk and look at the forest again.)

I didn't have to venture very far, of course. Religious fundamentalism has become more and more of a driving political force, so the parallels between the current day and the political environment of Miller's seventeenth-century Salem were close enough to share train tracks—perhaps even more so than the Communist scare that had prompted Miller to write *The Crucible* in the first place. One could even say that the religious fervor on display in the script is no longer an allegory but a political reality. That might be painting with a broad brush, but it keeps that tantalizing question out there: If this culture had survived intact for four centuries, what would its adherents look like now?

We do have our contemporary versions of Miller's Puritans: Mennonites, Huttites, other nontechnology-based agrarian societies. These are very tightly controlled, almost closed-off societies, with limited involvement with the "outside world." They stay close to their own, as much as they possibly can. Their attire is very severe and slightly archaic, even though it relies on a few modern-day influences. They make almost all their own clothes: simple yet sturdy farm clothing, in severe colors, dark blues and blacks. The dresses are designs that harken back to the late 1800s, with long sleeves and long skirts of heavy, durable fabrics. Even their going-to-church wardrobe starts from this base, usually only adding a jacket to the men's outfits and a demure bonnet to the women's. There was our costume approach—simple, straightforward, no nonsense. The resulting design is a combination of shapeless overlays, blue jeans, work shoes, and broadcloth shirts, with lines that mix a contemporary rural look with an almost medieval gloss. The only affectation to indulgence comes in the robes of the judges (in this production, played by women), which are a rich velvet pile, held in place by a wide leather strap that snaps in the back. What was interesting about those, from a design perspective, is that they made the judges look like "one of the people" while at the same time pointedly reminding everyone that they were higher in the social order. A fine point, but a telling one.

Now that I knew who these people were, it was time to look at the world they lived in.

The set had to be visually austere and yet at the same time intellectually complex. Stark. Rigid. Very controlled. Empty and heartless. This extended the design into the idea of a "societal prison," from which there would be no discernible escape. From there, it was easy to see a closed box, which, prisonlike, would certainly fit with the themes of the play. But even though this was a prison of sorts, it couldn't look like one, at least not immediately. I needed to make its simplicity misleading: what would be open and spare at the beginning would become tight and confining at the end. Coupled with that, the props and furniture had to be almost geometric in their arrangement, as though *everything* onstage existed along a grid we couldn't see. A chair wouldn't be placed just anywhere. It had to have a specific place, one so defined that, were it off by only a few inches, you'd realize it. Even though you'd be hard-pressed to say exactly why, you'd say to yourself, "That doesn't look quite right."

In some respects, this is a very Zen-like design, where the minimalism speaks via the viewer's interpretation of the placement of the presented elements. There's a famous sand garden in Japan that's designed in such a way that you can never see all its rocks at the same time. You have to move around the space in order to capture it in its entirety. I wanted that same kind of complex minimalism in *The Crucible*: you might be able to see everything, but you couldn't see everything. Some elements might be just near enough to offstage to be slightly hidden, while others would be presented without explanation. There would be omitted details that the audience had to bring to the table to complete the visual experience. The danger, however, lay in not knowing how simple and barren I could make it before it became virtually nonexistent.

At the same time, the more I worked with this, the more museum-like it became, and that seemed a direction worth taking. Conceptually,

Inside the house.

museums are interesting places, displaying a few remnants of what were, without question, highly developed and complex societies and cultures. Limited by space, the act of displaying something like a chair fairly screams its own sense of self-importance, as though this single item could represent everything about an era and its people. But there's also a certain underlying self-mockery that says, "As a piece of furniture, this chair wasn't all that useful. Had it been, by now it would have been worn out through use. It's probably the least comfortable thing you'll ever sit in, which is precisely why it's still around." It's almost as if these items have survived because of their very uselessness, and I found that possibility intriguing, given the play and our approach to it. A society that hasn't changed all that much in four hundred years would have a stagnant, frozen, useless sense of self. But was that enough?

Almost. In addition to its museum-like quality, this was also becoming our "Robert Wilson" production, as Scott and I would joke later on. Wilson is a brilliant visual director, with a nearly inscrutable yet riveting theatrical sense. His productions are remarkably static in composition, with movements that take minutes, sometimes even hours, to complete—in one, an actress takes a full hour to prepare and pour a cup of tea. You'd think such indulgence would be relentlessly boring, but instead it has a near-mystical quality to it. Time slows down, allowing you to immerse yourself in the moment. And, more than anything else, there's an almost mechanical precision to it all. That intrinsic rigidity was precisely the atmosphere I wanted for *The Crucible*. Not that I wanted an already long play to extend to the length of a Wagnerian opera, but Wilson's method of treating actors like statuary was right in keeping with my "museum" approach to the design.

Ultimately, this distilled down to a deceptively calm box of delphinium blue. Why blue? you might ask. Gray was another possibility, but it would have been too obvious a choice. Remember: blue is a calm, dispassionate color. Other hues carried too much supplemental emotional baggage. But blue, particularly this specific shade of blue, felt neutral to the point of being only slightly unpleasant. Normally, we expect blue to be inviting, even nurturing . . . but blanketed over the entire set, it changed into something almost numbing to behold. With the costumes equally shaded and predominantly blue, characters would almost disappear into the walls, creating an image of a society without any real visual texture. Things—and people—would simply melt into each other, becoming a mass with no real definition, an ocean you could easily drown in.

Talk about scary.

(At this point, let's return to the costumes, just for a moment. Early in our discussions, Scott and I considered how the "witches" would appear in such a world. My instinct said we should put them in typical teen street wear, in colors that would jar with the relentless blue of the production, throwing them as far outside the "community" as we possibly could. The styling wouldn't be that different, remember, since everyone is in modern dress. But putting the girls in clothes we accept as conventional and then, without any changes, making them threatening would underscore the idea of mindless paranoia.)

The sides of the box had hinged panels that would swing out toward the audience to redefine the landscape but still prevented any visual sense of escape. Built from stock four-by-twelve and four-by-eight flats, the box required merely a couple of luan pieces for the upstage "teeth" and a coat of paint. Added to that were a few pieces of furniture: a bed and a few chairs defined the first scene. But it was the placement of these items of furniture that defined everything: set with mathematical precision, they, along with the actors, would give the room an almost sculptural yet melancholy feeling.

As such, this became a very spare, very architectural design, where motionless actors become plastic scenery: some are silent witnesses to the tragedy played out before them, while others are completely detached, evocative of the Puritan practice of "shunning." In the prison scene, for example, the design calls for a row of ladder-back chairs against the upstage wall. The people sitting there would do nothing, just watch. But it was to be left ambiguous: were these condemning townsfolk? Or others who had been accused, now waiting for their time before the judges? The design didn't comment either way; it was left for the audience to decide.

In the middle of act two, the world of the play cracks, literally: the back wall rips open to a black chasm for the judges' entrance, accomplished by sliding the pieces of the wall as far offstage as the limited wing space would allow. But normalcy is restored in the final scene: the box is now again unbroken, and the prisoners are trapped inside square lights that define the individual cells as well as mirror our sense of the outside world. Rigid order has been restored and maintained.

The Trial.

The jail cells, each defined by its own box light, with the row of chairs lining the upstage wall.

 The Crucible is arguably the most "Euro" design I've ever done for Scott. It has a distinctly different vocabulary, and some of its design concepts proved challenging for a high-school audience. But it was also one of their most successful productions, even more so than some of the musicals. It takes Miller's play into a landscape so devoid of emotion that nothing is left but an arid intellectualism—and it is this very emptiness of thought that, in the end, closes in and defeats the characters.

Guys and Dolls

Damon Runyon meets Ruby Keeler and Tom Wolfe

When Scott mentioned *Guys and Dolls* as a possibility for the one-act ccompetition, it was the first of many times I've said to him, "You're crazy." (Now it's practically a running joke: "You want to do what???") But working on *Guys and Dolls* turned out to be, for me, a breakthrough design. It convinced me that any show, no matter how big, could be condensed into manageable, bite-size pieces. All it took was finding a single focus that would support the entire script.

("All it took"? Yeah, right.)

First impressions are the most lasting, so, if you will, please consider just the scenic requirements: Times Square. A street off Times Square. Outside a Salvation Army church. Inside a Salvation Army church. The Hot Box. Havana. And top it all off, down in the sewers for the big crap game. There's a few more, actually: all the in-one scenes that were written originally so stagehands could change the scenery behind the curtain, a luxury not available to us. A frighteningly big show. And Scott needed to perform this in less than fifty-five minutes, with a set that could be transported in a small van (again!), along with the props and costumes. As with *Forum*, he managed to cut it down to the essentials of the script and four of the best-known songs, but we were still traveling all over New York as the play moves from scene to scene.

Absolutely crazy.

Still, I was game, so I read the truncated script, rented the DVD of the movie, and then started researching New York of the 1930s. Conveniently, when Scott assigned this, I planned to be in New York on a work vacation, so research meant going outside with a digital camera. How easy is that?

You can still see a lot of that era, especially around Midtown, specifically in the Fashion District and the area just east of Times

Square: the brick and concrete layout on the five- and six-story office buildings that line the areas off Broadway and Seventh Avenue, even the typographic layout of the faded window signs in the delicatessens. For all the rebuilding done in Times Square, there's a lot of Damon Runyon's New York still standing. It feels very gray, all of it: gray concrete, gray brick, gray plaster, gray signs. But all that gray gives what color remains in the signs a lot more pop, which might suggest one reason why we look at them and find them so relatively garish. Still, if my set were going to be predominantly monotone (and I already suspected it would be), I'd need that garish coloring somewhere.

When he was working on the great New York musical *Company*, designer Boris Aaronson said he spent one entire day just counting the number of buttons he pushed to get somewhere in Manhattan. I did a similar exercise, counting the number of times I crossed Forty-second Street duirng a single day in Midtown. It was a lot. I wasn't surprised: New York, after all, is about people on the move, everyone trying to get somewhere, either geographically or professionally. But as you move through Manhattan, there's a strange visual shift that happens as you walk past buildings. You discover you use landmarks such as the Empire State Building or the Woolworth Building to orient yourself. Their positions in relation to other skyscrapers tells you more than just simple east or north. You know neighborhoods by the arrangement of the skyscrapers in the background: a particular order tells you, you are in Chinatown or the Theatre District or the West Village.

In addition, walking along, say, Thirty-fourth Street gives you the odd sense that the laws of perspective have decided to go to Coney Island for the afternoon, leaving buildings to move horizontally as you walk past. They do, of course, but it's as though they've collapsed down to two dimensions, height and width, with depth off in Brooklyn enjoying a hot dog and a roller-coaster ride. A friend of mine calls this the Viewmaster effect, in reference to the later Viewmaster reels—not the ones shot with stereopticon cameras but those with the "false" 3D effects. With the false ones, you take photos and lay them on pieces of clear glass or plastic, then take a picture. Then you move the layers a bit and reshoot, then set up the images so that each eye looks at only one and your brain puts them together. Done properly, the combined

The basic Guys and Dolls set. The groundrow and header were cut from the touring production, but note how they create an interesting shadow array on the backdrop.

images create a false sense of 3D. While the stereo view is truer, the false 3D is more interesting, perhaps because it requires the viewer to put something into it in order for it to work. It's like looking at Restoration stage scenery: you know it's just wings and drops, but it looks like something else. Not quite a fully realized room, but not quite not one.

The idea that the architectural topology shifted in this flat-yet-not kind of way seemed a likely starting point for the design. Much of the show takes place around Times Squares, which suggests that any street-level view of the surrounding skyscrapers would be defined by your relationship to the nearest tall building, whether the Chrysler or the Empire State. Both of those would have been under construction during Damon Runyon's time, and being so much taller than anything surrounding them, both would have been clearly visible for blocks in any direction. With that in mind, I wondered if it was possible to show the movement from one place to another—not flats rolling off and scrims flying in, but actual movement, as though the characters were walking through the canyons of Manhattan. That in turn sparked the memory of Ruby Keeler singing "Forty-Second Street" and the dancing chorus of cardboard buildings behind her.

The Hotbox, with its footlights. Again, this changes the shadow pattern on the cyc.

The ah-hah moment: A miniature landscape for these big rollers to walk through? Runyon meets Tom Wolfe's Masters of the Universe?

(Hello, key. Thanks for stopping by.)

That sounded like fun, so my first draft showed skeletal skyscrapers with oversized neon signs that would indicate the various scenes in the play. Built on little wagons, we could reconfigure these into any arrangement we wanted, even during a scene, to create an ever-changing skyline. To indicate where we were, an actor would flick on a switch, and a portable battery pack would light up a specific sign.

Great in concept, but a horror in execution: these would be top-heavy—never a good idea. Add to that, neon tubing is fragile, not to mention expensive for custom work. We explored the option of fiber optics, but those didn't give off the brightness I needed, so that idea died early in the discussions. Still, the movable miniature buildings were an idea definitely worth salvaging: I pushed it a bit further by emphasizing the contrast in height—originally, all of them were about five feet tall, but now they would range from six feet high to ten. Simple lateral shifting would give us far more variations of layout than we could ever possibly use. Rather than solid gray, I added details in silver (using that great old standby, silver duct tape) and black (that other old standby, electrician's tape). Put them onstage, and there you have it: a

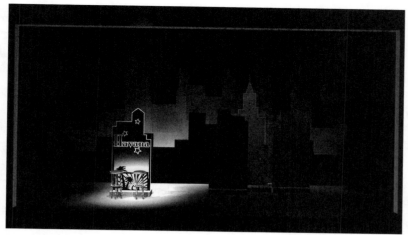

Havana.

mini-Manhattan. But we still had the issue of how to tell the audience where we were.

The solution was kick-yourself-in-the-head simple: turn the buildings around. All the reverse sides save one were dedicated to specific scenes, identified by painting large marquee-style signs in garish colors for everything from the Hot Spot to the Save-a-Soul Mission. Depending on the scene, we only added a few benches or a table with two chairs or a couple of stools, and the scene was complete. The result was flexible, fast, and fun for the cast as well as the audience.

The costumes were heavily inspired by the film *Dick Tracy*. The bold colors and clean, cartoon lines were right in line with the set, so it seemed a perfect marriage. We worked everything down to an eight-color palette, reserved two of them for our lead couples, and then distributed the remainder throughout the rest of the cast. There were no patterns, just bright swathes of solid color so everyone would look big.

(Rule of thumb number 23: You want someone to look small? Put your actor in a pattern. Big? Solid color. Works every time.)

All our men except Sky wore the same style: a long Zoot suit ensemble, with baggy pants, high waists, suspenders, coordinated wide ties, and fedoras. Sky's was slightly more conservative, with a suit vest, to reflect his more urbane position within the gambler hierarchy. As befitting his name, his outfit was blue based, but slightly deeper and darker than everyone else's. Nathan's ensemble was a cool purple, to associate him with Sky and yet put him slightly out of Sky's sphere.

This created a color progression that extended to everyone else in the show. The closer a particular character was to Sky, the closer his suit color was to blue. Cool violet? Forest green? You were high up in the hierarchy. Now move a little further away chromatically. Red? Yellow? You were a grunt. The women started from a basic dress: a full skirt hemmed below the knees, with a full bodice or blouse. They were then given accessories—belts, hats, and gloves—to pull their individual characters away from the pack. Our female leads were put in the same colors as their male counterparts, and the women's chorus was coordinated with the men's, even if people weren't partnered off in strictly defined couples.

The effect of all of that color against those silver and gray buildings was dazzling, yet controlled. Even with the full rainbow onstage (my friend Jim Lindsey describes the show as "like a box of crayons exploded up there"), you could still quickly locate the principals, but full-company numbers like "Rocking the Boat" were visually joyous and exciting.

A basic men's costume is created, then modified to change the color of the suit and hat. The individual renders are assembled into one image to test the overall color impact.

(Just a technical note: This was also the first time I explored "virtual costuming," design work created entirely on the computer. Because everyone would start from a basic outfit, I used a program called Poser to create a typical male and female outfit, then quickly sorted out colors by changing the color of the "materials zones" for the coat and pants and so on. Then I could take these and group them to study the overall effect. Working this way, I had almost the entire cast costumed in about fifteen minutes. I could even place them "onstage" in the set model so we could study them under lights.

When costumes came back from Scott for revision, I could pull up the image while we talked on the phone, make the requested changes, and send it down via the Internet for approval before we'd hung up. It's not a method that works for every show, but it was tailor-made for this one.)

The field of silver-gray on the buildings also affected stage composition in a surprising way. The costumes, as noted, were all pure color, so when we had a small scene, the mass of gray behind the actors allowed the stage focus to shutter down, like a movie close-up. And although they were small, we made sure there was always overlap in the arrangement of the buildings to keep that sense of a moving, changing mass. As a result, you focused on the scene, not the set. Sometimes it's nice to know that a dour old lady like Gray can still perform in a musical comedy when you want her to.

Put together and thrown into motion, this became a *Guys and Dolls* that was more about the characters than New York. Some folks might consider that heresy—after all, Runyon wrote his stories as a valentine to the Manhattan of that time—but it worked for us just fine.

Annie

Life in black and white

If any musical has bedeviled and frustrated me, it's *Annie*.

Annie is, of course, based on the famous Harold Grey comic strip, first published in 1924. He drew the panel until his death in 1968, at which point the distributor tried to continue by rerunning some of the older ones until 1979. After the success of the musical, different artists and writers tried to recreate Grey's achievement, with only limited success. It's told through the eyes (well, at least onstage she has eyes) of that curly-topped orphan and her dog that are as much a part of our national consciousness as hot dogs and apple pie.

It's also a sprawling monster of a show: a huge cast with serious scenic and costume demands. But we had to figure a way to whack it down to size; Scott was taking it to the one-act competition, and we were bringing it on the success of *Forum* and *Guys and Dolls*. It was probably one of the largest contingents of student actors Washington County had ever sent for a single production. Expectations were high all around.

I knew the show, mostly through the movie, but I had only a passing acquaintance with the original comic. A chance visit to a used bookstore garnered me a collection of the earlier strips—storylines that saw Annie less as an orphan in the storm and more like a gritty, homespun Nancy Drew. This particular anthology, from the 1930s, picks up her life after she left the orphanage and began her travels from one small town to another. Her faithful dog Sandy at her side, Annie solved mysteries and beat up neighborhood bullies while going to school, delivering newspapers, and (in her seemingly copious spare time) opening a novelty shop, which she then turned over to the poor family who took her in at the beginning of the saga. I assume that in subsequent volumes she finally arrived in New York and continued her sporadic life with Daddy Warbucks. Her time there would prove even more exciting, as the 1940s saw her blowing up Nazi U-boats while somehow managing never to age as much as a single day.

(The reason she never aged? According to Annie, it was because she was born on leap year day, which meant she aged one year in four.)

Reading just this one collection, I quickly saw that the philosophy of self-reliance and picking one's self up by one's own bootstraps was elevated to near religious fervor within the world of Little Orphan Annie. I have no doubt that during the Depression Era, the relentlessly cheerful yet pragmatic Annie (who was originally a boy named Otto until the strip's distributors convinced Grey that a girl might have broader appeal) was a courageous role model for millions of Americans who had no jobs and no homes and no hope. Many of the supporting characters in the early strips were the working poor and homeless vagrants, but few were played for comic relief: they were almost all proud, indomitable folks determined not to be broken down by circumstance. There were villains in the strips, but they were a curious lot: the idle, self-indulgent rich or the shady businessmen or the fast-buck con artists, people who used and abused the underclass, as opposed to the hardworking heroism and near-fatuous integrity of the super-rich entrepreneur Warbucks.

(Names in the strip went well beyond the symbolic. "Warbucks" alluded to the source of Daddy's amazing wealth, but we also had the impoverished family mentioned earlier, the Futiles, as well as the evil Pinchpennies. There was also the God-like Mr. Am; more on his mysterious powers later.)

In researching the strip, I found not only a unique visual style but also a great deal about the stylist himself. A brass-tacks ultraconservative in the truest sense of the word, Grey was almost an Ayn Rand–style Objectivist. He wanted nothing to do with the government, and he expected the government to reciprocate the favor. As far as he was concerned, the Depression would be over in a week if people just got over themselves and went to work. There were fortunes to be made, but you wouldn't make them by whining for a handout. As befitting a comic-strip artist, the ironically named Grey's worldview was very black and white; within it, people were either very, very good or very, very bad.

(Grey would have been appalled by the musical adaptation, if for no other reason than his personal loathing for Franklin Roosevelt and the New Deal. One of the ongoing plot devices in the strip was Daddy's disappearances as he foiled yet another scheme to harm Annie. These were harrowing cliffhangers, suggestive that Warbucks had narrowly averted some terrible end. But in one, Grey expressed his disgust with FDR by actually killing Warbucks off, only to have Mr. Am resurrect him when Roosevelt died.)

Although his lettering was shaky at best, Grey's naïve drawing style for the dailies the panel strips that ran from Monday to Saturday, was notable over time for its composition: he saw each panel as a canvas and laid on white and black with sensitivity and precision. He created shade and tone by exacting penwork, not Benday dots, and his stylized characters are comfortably and confidently rendered. The Sunday strips, by contrast, were wild profusions of color, with stark blocks of red and blue and green. No doubt tinted by another artist, they lose something in saturation because of the process of printing color on newsprint, but they make up for it with their high-contrast juxtapositions of complementaries. Sunday comics also commanded a full page, allowing Grey room to not only explore each panel's artistic potential, but all of the panels in concert as well—not to mention for the sometimes enormous amounts of dialogue between his characters.

Above all, Grey was a master storyteller, with tales that stretched for months, if not a full year, at a time. His politics were brandished for all to see, but his characters were so engaging and heartfelt that you were immediately hooked into the plot. No matter how absurd some of it might be—a regular secondary character was the eight-foot-tall behemoth Punjab, Warbuck's devoted, vaguely East Indian manservant, who used a magic cape to make miscreants disappear, permanently— you cared. You cared about Annie's never-ending stories of woe. You cared about Uncle Dan, the indigent violinist who befriended Annie and briefly made her a star in vaudeville before the exploitative producer smashed their dreams like so many cheap china plates. And because you cared, you stayed with it, no matter how long it took for Grey to spin the story.

I suggested to Scott early on that we might look at this production

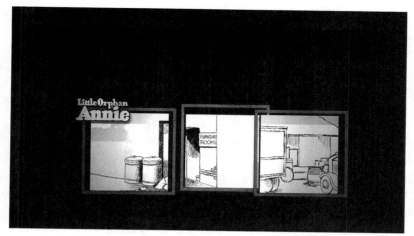

The basic comic-strip set.

as a tribute to Grey and the now-lost art of the comic strip, a concept he quickly embraced. To set the tone, each of the first ten scenes would be presented in black and white strip form, while the concluding eleventh, the Christmas party, would be our Sunday edition. In theory, this was highly workable: the black and white scenes would be presented using simple panel backgrounds that emulated Grey's drawings, which would keep scenery and props to a minimum and give the students a relatively simple task in scene painting. Easily moved, these panels would be set behind stationary, open square frames, which gave us something to suggest doorways and other entrance points. The Sunday panel would transform the stage into full color, giving the audience a visual payoff as well as a plateful of eye candy.

The panels had little referents built into them: each was dated, as comic strips are, and the observant audience member would see the subtle progression to December 25. Grey's unmistakable signature appeared on the color display. Finally, to give the visual equivalent of a daily strip becoming a full-page Sunday comic, we would have the Sunday panels on flats that were twice as high, with the upper array showing the characters of Annie, Daddy, and Sandy as they appeared in the strips (and in a bridging sequence that would delicately connect scenes 10 and 11). This would be accomplished by having the Sundays facing upstage, with their supporting framework painted as dense and deep a black as possible to hide them in front of the black velvets, then revolving on casters into position.

The costumes would follow suit, with everyone in black and white until the last scene, where we would finally see, among other things, Annie's famous red dress. In the dailies scenes, I allowed myself the option of using gray in the costumes, lest the stage become too stark, but even that gray had to be carefully chosen. Working with so-called neutrals, like black and gray, you quickly realize that there's really no such thing as a pure black or a pure white: they're either a bit blue or a bit brown. And if you mix a warm black with a cool one on the same costume, the result is as noticeable and jarring as blending orange and teal. Gray is even more elusive as the same gray will look different under different lights. Still, the first sketches looked promising—as well as intriguing: whether consciously or unconsciously, the design was quickly falling along color lines, white for the good people, black for the bad. Daddy Warbucks might be wearing a black tuxedo for the "NYC" number, but the white greatcoat and fedora would remind us that he was indeed a good person. The costume colors for the finale were designed with as much visible contrast as their newspaper counterparts. All in all, a production that would be, for its size, relatively inexpensive, easily transported, and conceptually unique. It seemed we had our design key, one that acknowledged the musical's comic-strip origins as well as Grey's straightforward and sometimes simplistic worldview.

You notice that, two paragraphs up, I said that in theory this was workable. But once I started designing the particulars, problems raised their ugly little heads. First was the sheer number of background panels, even for a truncated version of the show that had repeating locales. Then, the double-high flats had to fold down for transport and yet easily flip back up for performance. Some furniture pieces, like Warbucks's desk and Hannigan's radio, could be built as two-dimensional cartoons, but others, such as the orphans' beds and all the chairs for the cabinet, simply had to be there—somehow.

There's a lot of furniture in *Annie*.

To address the quantity of black and white panels, I revised the design schema so that some scenes required merely a single panel and

The double-high, full-color Sunday edition.

others no more than two—this eased the construction and also provided a means of shifting the focus from scene to scene. Aside from the finale, only once in the show—during "NYC"—did I have all three frames in use. Next, the panels were built on a double-sided chassis that reduced the number of panel wagons, making offstage storage and sequencing much easier to control. The full-color double highs were piano-hinged and then locked into position with a carriage bolt before placement onstage.

Scott suggested we not have anything for the beds, just thin gray blankets on the floor that the orphans could use as choreography props for "Hard Knock Life." That worked for me. As for the chairs for the cabinet scene, we realized they could do double duty in the Warbucks mansion as well as the radio scene, so it seemed that issue was taking care of itself.

The show was distilling very nicely at this point. Still, there was a larger conceptual issue I hadn't anticipated. The panels worked, but they were also (to me anyway) annoyingly predictable. The set was calling attention to itself by being exactly what we wanted it to be. Granted, we were trying to make everything look like comic strips, which are about as two-dimensional as it gets, but there was something missing. All the pieces were there, just not quite in the right place.

The second take: slightly more successful, but still not quite there.

Ironically, another comic artist of the same period provided at least part of the answer. Will Eisner, the author/illustrator of the classic Spirit comics, wrote that in good sequential art the action isn't in the panels but between them. For example, in one panel, you might see the Spirit, a hard-nosed detective, looking behind him as he cautiously entered a building. In the next, he would be pounding on someone's door. What you didn't see was his running up the three flights of stairs to get there.

That set me to wondering if maybe I wasn't being a little too rigid in my approach to the comic-strip concept, that perhaps we could safely move from it without hindering the basic idea. Again, all the pieces were there; maybe I just had to rethink the composition a bit.

Maybe it was simply a matter of shifting things over and sliding them around, so the action would take place between the panels.

Truly, it was that easy, even though it took more time to see the obvious than you'd think. But having the panels straddled between frames suddenly gave the stage picture the texture and depth it was missing. We were back on track.

Well, almost.

It still didn't feel quite right, although we were at a loss to say what was wrong. And we were running out of time.

The production went to the one-act competition and took a disappointing third in regional, which basically shut it out from going to state. It wasn't anyone's fault: the cast had performed its best and then some, and the production looked smart. The problems went much deeper than that. Once again, the pieces were all there, just not in the right places. Like dealing with some sort of infernal Rubik's cube, we could see all the parts, and we knew what the solution was supposed to be, but the process to get there remained tantalizingly out of reach.

As a concept, *Annie* never quite jelled, and I put this case study in here as an example that not everything works like you hope it will. While the core idea and the design key were there, we hadn't really delved deep enough into them, and the result was a production that, while perfectly acceptable, wasn't quite to the standard we'd intended it would be. Still, in the end, Scott and I consoled ourselves that it was work well done and that the students enjoyed the experience, and we moved on to the next project.

(Ironically, the night I sent Scott the final working drawing and paint elevations, I went to bed at 3 AM convinced I'd backed everything up on a CD before deleting the files from my computer. I got up the next morning to find that only the initial studies were intact; everything else was now lost in the electronic ether. Maybe I should have seen that as a sign.)

A brief coda to all this: two years later, I got the opportunity to try again, with a company that had seen the design on my web site and wanted to use it. I explained to the director what went wrong and revised the schema to correct what I thought were some of the problems. Rather than tightly binding itself to the comic-strip format, this version used it as a touchstone for something more of a fantasia on the conceit than a literal reproduction. It worked a little better the second time around, in part, I'm sure, because I allowed myself the freedom to use the format as a starting point, not a final destination. Nevertheless, I hope that one of these days I'll get a third crack at it. Like Annie herself dealing with dog-nappers and Nazis, I'm resolutely certain the solution is there if I just work at it hard enough.

Fools

transforming a man into a giant chicken

Fools is a fun play to design, no bones about it. Set in Russia around 1900 (but, as you'll see, not for long), it tells the story of a schoolteacher who arrives in a village under a supposed curse of stupidity. A cautionary fairy tale about the power of self-awareness, it has some of Neil Simon's most stream-of-consciousness writing, with hilarious word associations that seemingly spring out of nowhere.

Like *Forum*, it has an almost "presentational" sensibility about itself, with a narrator and a cast of stylized characters. It takes edits very easily, which made it a great prospect for the one-act competition. With only two locales—a village square and inside a doctor's house—it's not especially demanding. Once Scott finalized it as his choice, I was off and running.

As I read the first act, I tried to figure out a specific reason why Simon set it in 1900. It's not quite pre-Revolution, and there's nothing in the dialogue that suggests any eminent political changes on the horizon. It was written too early to be a parody of Y2K. And from a visual point of view, it's not an especially picturesque era, particularly when a good chunk of the cast are peasants. So woolgathering kicked in.

A village under a self-imposed curse that has apparently been around for a couple of centuries. People living under a self-perpetuating cloud of superstition and a baseless fear of education and knowledge. Did that seem historically familiar? Like maybe the Middle Ages? It is a fable, after all, and some of the best come from that once-upon-a-time—especially in Russia, where the storytelling tradition runs very deep. Tales like "The Snow Queen" and characters like Babba the Hut (a log house that walks around on chicken legs) only slightly suggest the strange and wondrous world of Russian folktales.

In the process of researching the visuals, I discovered Russian illustrators whose drawings of those folktales defined the subject matter almost as much as Gustav Doré defines our interpretation of *The Divine Comedy*. Russia was blessed with some amazing illustrators around the period 1900 to 1940, not the least of whom is Ivan Bilibin. His style (governed by the printing processes of the time) set the standard, it seems, for everyone else, with its recognizable black outline and solid color fill. He used color so artfully and daringly that the result is something of extraordinary complexity. His work, no matter what the medium, has a sophisticated folktale sensibility, even those that are supposed to take place in cosmopolitan St. Petersburg, and all of it has an aura of magic and wonder. His books are all retellings of Russian folk tales, like "Vassilisa the Beautiful" and "The Frog Princess," while his theatre work graced the premieres of *Sadko, Petroushka,* and *The Golden Cockerel*. Most notable are the borders of his full-page illustrations, with their combinations of geometrics and legendary beasts and deep, dense forests. It's a style that seemed perfect for Simon's spellbound village, so I happily dove into Bilibin's collected works, finding anything and everything that would speak to my cast of folktale characters and their world.

The deeper I looked, the more enchanting it became. With its boyars and princesses and shepherds and knights, Bilibin's work would give me a predominantly Byzantine and Asia Minor approach to the costumes, with massive, colorful robes, wildly feathered hats, and layer upon layer of skirting. I could also toss in a few East European influences for the schoolteacher, mix all the ingredients well, and serve up a production schema that had color, style, and more than a little self-conscious wit.

(I know, I know: "He's playing with the author's intentions again!" Well, not quite. Yes, I'm shoving it back in time a couple of centuries, but not out of whim. OK, not entirely out of whim. The chosen time period would definitely support the themes in the script: ignorance is bliss, knowledge is to be feared. If anything, these ideas were far more prevalent in the Middle Ages than the turn of the century that Simon specifies, so why not give them air to breathe and room to grow into whatever lunacy they could?)

Analyzing the cast, you find that there are three distinct social

Left to right: Gregor, Magistrate, Sophia, Leon, Lenya, Zubritsky.

classes in *Fools*. At the top, the Count, who's so "evil" he doesn't even come across as villainous: he's a melodrama villain, one step shy of the curved moustache and the hand grasping the mortgage for the farm. Just below him are the bourgeoisie: the doctor, his wife, their daughter. Beneath them, the townspeople, the shepherd (or in our case, shepherdess), and the postman.

Were there postmen in the Middle Ages? you ask. To which I sneeringly reply: Does it matter? After all, this is Neil Simon we're dealing with here, not *Doctor Zhivago*. As long as we can make the postman look like he belongs, he will. And the audience will accept it.

To set the tone for the costumes, I decided that, as you ascend through the social strata, your attire becomes more and more outrageous—in color, in detail, in line. The wilder and fussier and more bizarre it is, the more you are someone of importance. Meanwhile, the lower classes might have clothing simpler in form but odder in its combination of textures. Nothing is especially sane. At the top of our world is the Count, whose bright yellow uniform with its long, flowing sleeves and high-plumed hat makes him look like an enormous chicken, not a member of royalty. At the bottom, the shepherdess, whose capelet was made from neon pink sheep's wool. And into the middle of this wanders the relatively simple and contrastingly realistic costume of the schoolteacher. The moment he came onstage, you knew he didn't stand a chance with this bunch.

Because this was another touring production—it went to not only the one-act competition but also a drama festival or two—I had the same issues with the scenery that I did with *Forum*: something that would be easily packed, nothing too big, no problem with set up or tear down. So a styled minimalist look was the solution, with "nesting doll" panels upstage and Biliban-influenced borders on the sides. The village itself became a study in "reapplied perspective." A few small buildings, suggestive of log construction, were strategically placed to create a toylike sensibility. But all had hidden doors that allowed props and costume pieces to emerge, and all were strong enough to stand alone: both these features had the immediate effect of visual dislocation. To push the absurdity even further, a few sheep were added to the design—the missing flock everyone's looking for at the top of the play. As the performance continues, these sheep (which were built on little platforms) transform into chairs and sofas and tables and footstools. It's only at the end, when the curse is lifted, that everyone recognizes them as sheep once again.

The basic set. The "sheep" served as anything but sheep until the end of the play.

Transformation is the key here. The curse is gone, and everyone formerly stupid changes into someone . . . well, now not quite so stupid. But before that can happen, an inanimate sheep has to become a chair. A man dressed in his best clothes to woo his intended magically becomes a bird. And in the end, as the schoolteacher tell us, knowledge transforms everybody and everything. The more things change, the closer we come to the moral of Simon's endearingly silly little fable. And the more the set and costumes alter our perception of the story, the more they support it.

Stop for a Moment

Time TO COLLECT A FEW THOUGHTS.

Why do these productions work? Quite simply because they make their statement in one grand yet concise gesture. *Forum* is a commedia play. *Crucible* is a box. *Fiddler* is a campfire story. In all these, the design statement has been refined down to its most essential; anything that doesn't contribute to that has been disregarded.

Once more, this isn't about simplicity so much as distillation, reducing things to their most vital and communicative: the form that speaks the loudest, the line that is the most suggestive. In every case, there is the key, that one specific thing that exists to condense the play down to its most evocative: Zen design, if you will.

Zen uses an exercise called koans, for all intents and purposes riddles intended to focus the mind and develop intuitive thinking. In that spirit, here are a few questions you might ask yourself as part of the design process. At first glance, some of them will seem obvious—until you look again and realize there might be more than just the obvious answer.

- What is this play about?

- Is it a comedy or a tragedy?

- Who are the main characters? Describe them to yourself in detail: their personalities, their personal sense of style (or lack of it), their character quirks. How old are they? Does their age impact the look of the play? For example, what does *Glass Menagerie* look like if Laura is twenty? What would change if she were forty?

- If the character list is all men or all women, how does that affect your design choices and what would happen if you reversed the gender? For example, how would a female production of *Waiting for Godot* differ from a male production?

- When does this play take place? Don't say "the current day." Pin it down to a specific date, even if it feels arbitrary. For example, let's say *West Side Story* takes place on August 17, 1963. What is it about that specific date that you can use in your design? The summer heat? The visual sense of the early 60s? The fact that it was a Friday?

- If it's a single set, what room does the play take place in? Why in that particular room? If you changed the room, how would it change the play? For example, what would happen if you put *Crimes of the Heart* in the parlor instead of the kitchen?

- If it's a multiset play, what is there about the various locations that ties them together? For example, in *Fiddler*, it's all about the village. Metaphorically, what is a village?

- What is the "world" of the play, geographically, temporally, and socially? For example, is *Titus Andronicus* a Roman play or an Elizabethan play?

- Is there something about the play's historical or social heritage that might give it a new direction? For example, what was the original purpose of writing *Oedipus Rex*, and how does that specific purpose impact on the play?

- If the time in which the play is set is being changed, does the new time sufficiently parallel the original? For example, what would you have to do to make *School for Scandal* work as a modern-dress production? Do Sheridan's Restoration archetypes have contemporary counterparts?

- If the play is sparking a particular color in your mind, what happens when you look at that color's complement? For example, what would a green Harmonia Gardens restaurant look like? What would its effect be on the audience in telling the story of *Hello Dolly*?

- If the locale is being changed, are there geographic and social parallels that will make that move cohesive and logical? For example, would *A Cherry Orchard* work if set in South Africa?

- What happens if you tell the story backwards? For example, if you start from the fact that Willy Loman is going to die in a car accident, does that change your design approach?

All these should lead you to a final series of questions: What is the one visual element you need to establish your design? Why? What does its importance say about the play? This last one is the most crucial question of all because it informs you how the play will distill. It doesn't mean you're limiting yourself to just that one element, whatever it might be. Rather, it forces you to focus on the most essential piece of your design and to build out from there with economy and surety of vision.

Remember, these are just starting points. They're not a recipe or a road map, but rest assured that you can find the key somewhere in the answers. If it doesn't manifest itself in the time period's architecture, perhaps it's in the main character's choice of a sweater. Anything is possible, if you allow it. But trust yourself: the key is there, in every play and every musical and every opera. And once you find it, the design will fall neatly and elegantly into place.

PORTFOLIO STUDIES

The PRODUCTIONS THAT FOLLOW REPRESENT extensions of the ideas and concepts discussed in the case studies. They are divided into three sections: musicals, straight plays, and operas. With a few exceptions, they are all *big* shows that seem so daunting that you might be inclined to say, "No way." And when I say "big," I don't necessarily mean a big cast. A big show can also be one that has seemingly huge production requirements, even with a small cast. *Noises Off* only has eight characters, but that set can make a strong man weep.

Do not despair.

As you look at them and read the conceptual notes, observe how everything reduces to its most essential elements. The particular theatres mounting some of these plays had plenty of offstage room, which I certainly used, but all of them were—and still are—victims of a national economy that sees more and more regional companies falling on hard times.

And we designers are usually the first to feel the pinch.

And all the offstage room in the world won't solve that.

Note also some of the techniques used: the partial fly, for example. I won't pretend to have invented, let alone perfected, any of these, but they're systems that sometimes get overlooked because folks think, sometimes a little too adamantly, "Oh, I don't have a fly system; this won't work for me." It can, if you allow it. Just give yourself the liberty to explore the possibility.

Remember that some of these images are first passes and conceptual studies and, as such, might look a little thin. You're not looking for the final polished design here. That's not the point at this stage of the design game. Textures and details come later in the process; for now it's about communicating ideas to the director.

Finally, from an execution point of view, a few of these are pretty adventuresome: eate drops, mechanical effects, complicated constructions. That might seem to run counter to the idea behind this book, but once more, I ask you to look at them as extensions of the theory behind the designs done at Washington County. These demonstrate that not every *Beauty and the Beast* has to look like the Disney film and not every *Footloose* has to demand a full fly grid. They also show that even straight plays need not be locked down to the "expected": even classics like *Hedda Gabler* and *Hay Fever* can be approached afresh and made visually exciting. What we're ultimately driving toward here is a notion of how to work (and succeed) with a visual concept, how to toy with a scenic approach, how to pull tradition out of a rut—and in the process, save a few bucks along the way.

Musicals

Carousel

circles within circles

The stage arch at this is very wide and very high, designed for a balcony that was never built. Instead, the audience sits at floor level, which is set four feet below the deck and at an extremely gentle rake. There is no orchestra pit; instead, the musicians are put on the floor in front of the stage. As a result, sightlines are, to be kind, challenging at best. So a show like *Carousel*, which has a pretty hefty list of scenes, is approached with caution.

Another piece of "Euro" design, the look of this classic musical was built almost entirely around circles and curves and false perspective: the lighthouse is only ten feet high, but the forced perspective in scenes such as the park made it look twice that. The audience's low-set point of view also worked to our advantage, as it allowed me to create an artificial horizon line that was only about six inches above deck level, thus making the forced perspective work even harder. Stylistically, there's a vague sense of the old TV show *The Time Tunnel*, but the end result is something that constantly takes the viewer deeper and deeper into an unknown void.

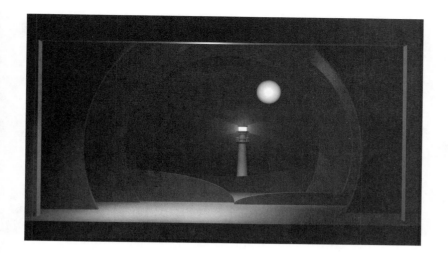

On the practical side, the neat thing about this essentially unit design is how well it hides everything in a theatre with no fly space and little wing space. The circles within circles allowed us to create deeper upstage wings for storage as well as partial flies for the Heaven scene's planets without sacrificing Hamden's huge picture frame.

Ironically, it's almost the same blue that I used in *The Crucible*. And it's interesting—to me, anyway—how the same color feels so uncomfortably dead in that production and so mysteriously hopeful in this one.

Peter Pan

mourning a dead mother

This approach to the tale of the boy who never grows up started from thinking first about what it was like to be a kid in a typical upper-class Edwardian home. An army of nannies and nursemaids, not the parents, would care for the children. Their toys would be tin mechanicals and toy theatres and those slightly disturbing ceramic-faced dolls, but it would be through the world of their imagination that we discover Neverland.

One thing that struck me when first reading the script was how the adults talked, almost like children pretending to be parents. Look at the scene between Peter and Wendy in Neverland: they talk just like Mr. and Mrs. Darling in act one (and more obviously, act three). So what if Mr. and Mrs. Darling as presented in the script aren't the actual parents? Perhaps the actual parents are these momentarily seen shadows that come in at the beginning of the play to kiss the children good night and then disappear, leaving them to escape into and run wild in their imagination?

Or to go even more extreme, perhaps we set up something at the beginning to suggest the real mother is dead. It's just the father: this cold, distant, very proper man who has maidservants to tuck the children in. He stands at the door, but won't come into their lives. So the children, as children are wont to do, create their own idealized parents through playacting, which leaves an interesting layer on the Peter-marries-Wendy scene in act two. They may or may not remember their mother; if they do, it's in that rose-colored way we have when dealing with painful memories. So what if the kids use a pair of ceramic bride and groom dolls as Mr. and Mrs. Darling—dolls that "talk" and "walk" and in general interact via the children. Even the dog is a giant plushy toy the children manipulate. Maybe Princess Tiger Lily is the sugges-

Bedroom.

tion of their real mother, and maybe Hook is the father we saw in that prelude.

Then, in act three, rather than dolls, we see these two again, both dressed in "adult" versions of the bride and groom outfits—and somewhere along the way, the adults disappear, transformed back into dolls. Outside, the sun starts to rise, and only the father appears in the doorway to silently allow the maids back in to wake the children up for the day.

As I noted in the script when considering this concept: "This could be creepy."

Is it still *Peter Pan*? You betcha. Look deep enough, and this is a creepy story, period. Eternal youth, as Peter finds out too late, is a horrifying curse.

Much of this demands that the bedroom make an immediate and very pointed statement. One giant wall. A huge door upstage: when open, it shows a hallway. No windows. Not a drab prison, but not exactly a swell place either. But when Peter makes his appearance, he does so through the door, except now it's a dream-inspired window, with a hint of a full moon. Then, when we fly to Neverland, the upstage wall flies, revealing a gorgeous night sky.

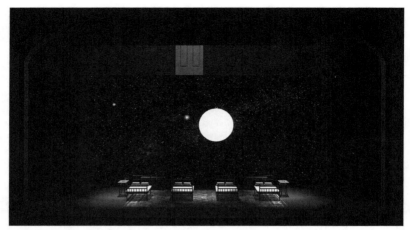

Flying.

(Heresy of heresies, I even suggested early on that we not have Peter fly into the bedroom, that his first appearance is from behind a bed—implying that he's always there with the children. As you might imagine, that went nowhere fast.)

Once in Neverland, the bedroom wall is still there, but everything's changed: just as a child will pull a blanket over himself to fashion a make-believe tent, things in the bedroom transform to become part of this larger, more fantastic world. The still-present back wall tilts at odd

Underground.

angles, revealing pieces of scenery, just enough to suggest, never quite enough to explain. We never let the audience forget where we are, that everything contained in this bedroom is part of the wonder of this strange world of the children's imagination.

Then, in the final scene, we're back in the bedroom, but it's twenty years on. Perhaps just as drab, but somehow more suggestive of home. Peter comes in through the window again, but not before we've first seen it as a door.

The Wizard of Oz

a yellow brick road that goes nowhere

This modernist take uses legs and undulating borders of vivid green as well as a curving platform upstage, and that's pretty well it. Within this, lightweight, conelike trees and a castered yellow ramp define Dorothy's stops on the way to the Emerald City, which itself is suggested by nothing more than a few sequined banners and a series of mobile, free-standing doors. In contrast, a jumble of vivid red telephone trees define the forest outside the castle of the Wicked Witch. It's all a little playful and a little surreal and a little unsettling all at the same time—unsettling because the set was purposely designed with as little a visual through-line as possible. Everything was left incomplete: the road goes nowhere.

But who hasn't seen *The Wizard of Oz* and asked him- or herself, What in God's name is Dorothy thinking? Going on what is most certainly a suicide mission just on the say-so of a talking head? Sure, she has a few friends with her, but based on her then-limited experience with them, who wouldn't be saying, "Uh, girlfriend, let's sit down and talk about this a bit, huh?" As such, our Emerald City—indeed, Oz in general—was as fragmented as the road getting there; in effect, I took away the romantic vision so that Dorothy would have one more reason not to stay. It's all very pretty, but it's not comfortable.

There were several visual moments worked into the design: a traveling tab panel that took us from the farm to Professor Marvel's wagon and back again, a ragged-edge gray scrim and whirligigs and rod puppets that danced across the stage during the tornado; a crescent moon that rolls across the upstage platform to reveal the witch's castle, a gigantic masklike costume for the Wizard that falls apart to become a simple robe upon his reveal. A very defined color palette: gray for Kansas, green for Oz, red for the Wicked Witch of the West—I figured I owed the audience at least that much tradition.

Kansas.

There was also the barely suggested hint of encroaching technology: the telephone poles outside and the giant clock inside the witch's castle were little grace notes that underlined the fear folks in the early 1900s had about such things running across their farmland. No wonder Dorothy is so disappointed in the wizard when all he can give her friends are gimmicks and toys instead of the very human attributes they seek.

Dark forest

Singing in the Rain

the magic of moviemaking

This particular company produces shows at a dinner theatre on a space that, like that utilized by so many of my clients, is crippled with a lack of facility. This one comes with a tiny thrust stage, minimal backstage, entrances and exits that can only happen from upstage right, no fly system, and a large set of nonfunctional roofing beams that visually clamp the stage down to about twelve feet in height. Most of their shows are pretty small productions: unit set, limited cast. But every now and then the director decides to tackle something big. *Damn Yankees. The Sound of Music. Best Little Whorehouse in Texas.* Large shows that, as with my work with Scott, sometimes left me thinking, "Huh? You want to do what?" But *Singing in the Rain* ran past the customary spatial problems into the realm of all new ones—not the least of which was the rain itself.

The bus stop. Note how it uses the old movie trick of a rear projected image.

The concept in this design was to treat the stage and the area immediately before it as a small soundstage. Movies in the 1930s were still little more than plays put on film, so I took that idea and built a space in which a film of *Singing in the Rain* is being shot as we're watching a performance of the stage play *Singing in the Rain*. The schema used all the tricks of early motion pictures, such as rear-screen projection for

When sound becomes the rage, the soundstage is covered in cable and hidden microphones.

The "elocution" scene.

the "Dancing Cavalier" scene. And there was something deliciously wicked about a film studio called Mammoth churning out these huge epics while working out of a space the size of a two-car garage. It took an extraordinary amount of preplanning because of the limited offstage space. Amazingly, in my computer model it all fit.

Still, as much as the director loved it, the producer turned it down and asked for something completely different. The final design was pretty cool, using the motif of "the silver screen" as an omnipresent background. Rather than set everything on a soundstage, now it was a 30s Deco theatre, where castered banks of theatre seats and a movie screen that split into rotating panels created the various scenes. It was definitely clever (and there's certainly nothing wrong with clever, not by half), but this first approach feels more like a celebration of the magic of moviemaking, where illusion is everything.

West Side Story

a playground of death

In contrast to the curves and soft tones of *Carousel*, this show at the same facility was a production design completely about hard, right angles, gritty textures, and high-contrast colors.

Playgrounds in New York are little more than asphalt with chain-link fencing—not exactly the best place for kids. But to softly underscore the fact that these are all kids onstage, I utilized the playground-fencing approach and added a few rented scaffolding units and some small furniture pieces to create the various scenes.

I wanted things in the air to keep the focus at deck level, so the solution was to create a rigging system that hangs pieces as high as possible, but leaves them somewhat in view, and then let them descend as needed. This series of partially (and separately) flown pieces of link fencing gave the Hamden proscenium a visual top, but when they

The prologue.

Maria's bedroom. Note how the number of scenic elements hasn't really changed, but now the stage seems tighter and more confined.

moved in staggered form from the fly rail to the deck, they not only al-lowed a variety of looks but also brought the eye down with them, in effect closing down the stage. Then, cluster the scaffolds, and you make a big stage suddenly seem small and intimate. By the same token, pull the fence panels as high as the rigging allows and shove back the scaf-folding—and the enormity of the stage becomes apparent once more.

There are also "negative borders": pieces of corrugated and scrap plywood that created, in reverse, a skyline. By changing the lights, we could go from a scene with an oppressive overhead weight to one with infinite stars.

Beauty and the Beast

Nature reclaiming its own

The contract that accompanies this show has the not-so-unusual clause in it that you are not allowed to do anything that resembles either the movie or the original stage production. That sounded fine to me, actually: anyone can copy the Disney movie. I wanted to experiment and see how un-Disney I could make it. So, script in hand, I started looking under the hood of the story for a few ideas.

If the people in the castle were slowly transforming into objects, I asked myself, what was happening to the castle? Reverting as well, of course: after all, if the spell changes the prince and his staff and his pets, not to mention the dishes and silverware, the castle itself also would seem to be on the hit list. But to what? Something natural, no doubt: just as the Prince loses his humanity, so would the castle and its environs lose their sense of man-made, artificial structure, much like abandoned houses slowly become part of the meadow. For a large

The various shields identify the merchants' trades in the village.

Lightning bugs illuminate the ballroom scene.

structure like a castle, something on an equal scale—old-growth forest, perhaps.

And suddenly the design fell into place: the castle was still vaguely a castle but now more like a gigantic storybook tree, similar to the colossal redwoods one sees in Muir Woods in northern California. That left open the opportunity for some lovely, decidedly non-Disney possibilities: the lights in the ballroom are courtesy a flock of lightning bugs. The window that defined Belle's room is covered with a canopy of flowers, while the West Wing resides uneasily in the branches. Sometimes rooms are inside the trunk and sometimes outside under its leaves. Hallways and doors are defined by massive, aboveground roots. Once-orderly rows of books change into a cascade of leaves that descend from the boughs overhead. There's the overwhelming sense of everything once architecturally defined in the castle becoming, well, something else entirely, less designed by man and more reclaimed by nature,

The books in the library become leaves in the tree.

just as the Beast and the objects are close to the final stages of their transformations—he to take his place in the forest as an animal, they to somehow share his fate through their own unresponsiveness at his intransigence (which I gather is the rationale for their changes). The area beneath the enormous arching roots serves as the dungeon, and the roots themselves provided a grand staircase between the deck and the upper levels. I looked to paintings by Eyvind Earle as a stylistic inspiration: he was the artist who provided the near-graphic backgrounds for *Sleeping Beauty*. Set inside a false proscenium of an open book, it was a design that resonated with the movie while making its own unique statement.

The design never got past this point, unfortunately. What we ultimately did was spectacular, had its own moments of ingenuity, and certainly showed off every penny we spent on it. But this one still seems a lot more interesting from a purely conceptual point of view.

Hello Dolly

Currier & Ives, postmodern

This was my second shot designing *Dolly*, actually. The first time was a spec design submitted to a dinner theatre in Calgary as a demonstration of what I'd do with their singularly awkward space. It had a full-stage revolve and four rotating mirrors that allowed pieces of the sets to circle into view from upstage. The tolerances between the sets and the mirrors were frighteningly slim—one slight move and things would crash into each other, sending hats and bags of feed and chicken dinners flying in all directions. It was never built.

Not so this time, I'm happy to report. The company for this production uses the stage at Washington County High School, so I was already familiar with the space when I took the assignment.

Dolly is a curious show—big, certainly, but not quite as big as you might think. There're really only three sets of any size: Vandergelder's

Vandergelder's store.

Irene Molloy's hat shop.

store, the millinery shop, and the restaurant. Everything else is "outside the restaurant," "Fourteenth Street," "a side street," "a jail cell," all of which can be conveyed with virtually no scenery. Yes, there's the train and the parade float, but with a little imagination, you can eliminate those completely. We did. It was good.

The Harmonia Gardens Restaurant.

But this is one of those plays where you read it and, without even thinking, say to yourself, "This is a red play." Part of that no doubt comes from overfamiliarity with Oliver Smith's original work, but there's also an energy that runs through it that can be conveyed in no other color but red. The portal and the various set wagons gave the show a subtly streamlined yet quasi-Victorian feel, with an interior arch that suggested etchings by Currier & Ives. The specific locales were sketched out with just enough detail to make them communicate, and everything on the individual wagons collapses down or folds up to store offstage in as tiny a footprint as possible, some as small as three by six.

Dolly's big entrance might not have had the grand staircase, but we still had her center stage with a center door fancy reveal, one that is seriously fancy. What more can a diva ask?

The Sound of Music

relentless control

Another production that used the Sandersville stage and its inherent lack of offstage storage, this one utilized a row of Robert Edmond Jones–style columns whose interior archways were filled with small window units or crosses or Nazi flags, depending on where the play we happened to be.

A very tight design, it took its cue from Maria's position vis-à-vis the world around her: no matter where she goes, it's all very controlled and regimented. This is an example where the visual rhythm of a set can tell the audience a great deal about the world of the musical—everything from the base architecture of the set to its furnishings and props is perfectly spaced and perfectly balanced and makes no allowances for people who like to sing in the mountains.

The convent.

The villa.

The singing contest.

(In this, our Maria sang "The hills are alive . . ." from the aisle in the audience, thus giving everyone a sense, no matter how slight, of that freedom she felt before entering her disciplined, well-ordered world.)

The heraldic shields impose that sense of respect for long-standing tradition, while the convent fence, with its point-top finials, subtly underscores the prisonlike atmosphere. The colors are also equally restrained and very architectural: granite grays and marble whites, making moments like the children's colorful "curtain" costumes all the more outlandish in contrast.

Jekyll and Hyde

running a maze in Hell

Designing for a company that runs four shows in rotating repertory, I had to do two things at the same time: give them a cost-effective production season and provide them with an overall schema that allowed all four shows to switch out quickly on a nightly basis. Fortunately, Jekyll's flats were such that they would work with another show that season—*Dames at Sea*—with no changes whatsoever: it was simply a matter of turning them around for the *Dames* act one "backstage."

The concept for the *Jekyll and Hyde* design came from two unlikely film sources: Derek Jahrman's *Edward II* and the silent classic, The *Cabinet of Dr. Caligari*. The former gave me the suggestion of wide expanses of roughly textured plaster walls, while the latter evoked the idea of dramatic uplighting to cast huge shadows on the performers. Then, two stair units (also culled from other shows that season) were added, such that our space could be a basement atory or the streets of London

Enormous shadows define Jekyll's London.

The ballroom, with its massive chandelier.

by only moving them forward, backward, or at a right angle to the doorways. The specific scenes, such as the ballroom or the atory, were supplemented with flown pieces—chandeliers and vaguely nineteenth-century "scientific" equipment—and a rearrangement of a few furniture pieces.

Caligari's Expressionist sense might seem obvious as a design source, but why, you may ask, Edward? Were I pressed to answer, I'd say that it comes from the script's dictum that so much of the play appear as demented as Hyde's state of mind. Hyde is a rat caught in some infernal maze, and he seeks only to escape it, by whatever means he can. No matter where he turns, however, it's always the same walls in

Jekyll's laboratory.

the maze, the same vision of Hell. Nothing is even close to comfortable here, not even his fiancée's home. Nor his own, for that matter; it's all very strange and unreal. The full-stage application of the texturing also underscores Jekyll's (and Hyde's) focus on the here and now. He doesn't look at the wallpaper or the brickwork pattern because they're unimportant to him. All he knows is that they're barriers to whatever freedom he seeks.

This is a production where the lighting is as key to the success of the design as the set. Although easily placed, the lights that create those monumental shadows are an intrinsic part of the expression of Jekyll's world. He is a man forever haunted by his own shadow.

My Fair Lady

stacks of books in a life in disarray

This space has a grand total of three working flies, which meant planning my drops with care. But more importantly than that, it meant the production had to have flexibility and lots of it.

I've always liked *My Fair Lady* because it's such a wonderful adaptation of Shaw, both the play and the playwright. Even though Lerner and Loewe seemed to think that Shaw would have preferred Freddy for Liza, I'm not so sure. This is an "intellectual love story," where Liza and Higgins meet as equals, and I'm sure George Bernard knew it even as he wrote it.

My take was to design this as an "intellectual ballet"—a look that would leave the stage as clear as possible for the verbal dance that played out on it. As was the case with Washington County High, the producing company didn't have a lot of money to spend, and as with

The embassy is a study in gold and silver.

Odd lights and a burning trash barrel create the night outside Covent Garden.

Forum, that worked in our favor. I was forced to keep everything simple and elegant and focused on the two characters at the center of the story. There are suggestions of Edwardian arches and a scrim wall that served as an in-one curtain and only as much furniture and propping as absolutely necessary.

Stacks of books and an out-of-place wicker chair in Henry's study.

One thing of which I'm proudest is Higgins's library because it tells us so much about the man with the briefest of gestures. Rather than shelf upon shelf of books, I put the books in haphazard piles around the stage—even more so than you see in the render—as though suggesting that he would pick one up at random, get what he needed, then leave it someplace else. He'd never find it again, of course, and this, like the location of his slippers, is a constant problem. But with those simple pieces, we can underline his near-arrogant impetuousness and hopeless disorganization.

There was also the subtle touch of having one of Mrs. Higgins's wicker chairs (which we see in her conservatory in the second act) showing up in the library and looking woefully out of place, as though Henry borrowed it for some now-lost purpose and never bothered to return it. As with the books, it was a small way of showing how lost Higgins was, how much he needed someone—if for no other reason than to keep his books straight and his slippers found. For all his macho bluster, Higgins needs someone to take control of his life.

Footloose

dancing in a germ-free environment

The last production in this particular venue before the theatre was gutted for remodeling, *Footloose* was designed for a playing space that was small and cramped (no surprise there) and had a back wall that not only curved left to right but top to bottom as well, a small piece of the dome that once housed a massive merry-go-round that previously lived in the space. It took three tries to get something that would work in such an awkward configuration, and yet the final design served the play well.

The interesting thing about *Footloose* is the sense that the towns-people seem to want a "germ-free" environment, one protected from "infection" from the outside world. Taking a cue from the shape of the back wall, I proposed covering it with large white flats that, on top, had an applied abstract grid. The effect was to close everything off into a

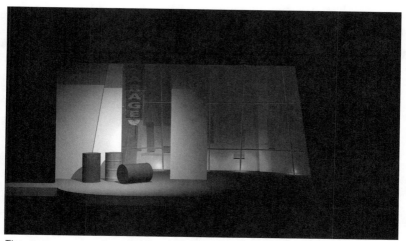

The garage, as antiseptically white as the rest of the town.

The roadhouse bar.

nearly sterile environment and allow no escape. This is different from the *Crucible* design, even though the goal appears to be the same. In this case, however, I wanted to give that suggestion that the outside world was coming in, come hell or high water. The grid would give the dancers something to hang from on occasion while also providing a bit of visual relief. At the same time, the cutouts in the flats could be neighbor windows or even something as simple as light pockets for the opening scene dance bar.

I relied on the partial fly again, this time to hide the signs for the

The bridge pylons.

burger joint and the eaves of the church. There were two traveling flats that provided "walls" as needed; behind them were the sign for the garage and a pop-up menu for the burger joint.

But my favorite scene in the design is the bridge. The script calls for the actors to be on top, but with this space, that was impossible—so I moved them to the base of the bridge and added two additional footers in false perspective. For storage, they were designed to nest like Russian dolls. Interestingly, while giving the scene a sense of distance and Midwest openness, they also had a vaguely funereal feeling.

Gypsy

life out of a suitcase

Anyone who's worked summer stock—or in theatre in general—knows that you live for months at a time out of a suitcase. It's not just some place to put your clothes and your toothbrush. It also becomes your living room, your office, your bedroom, and your "safe space."

So, for a show about itinerant showpeople, it seemed almost too easy to take the motif of the suitcase and blow it up to Ethel Merman–scaled proportions. There's a movable proscenium arch to remind us that this is a play about life in the theatre, but there's all these suitcases and trunks, both realistic and way overscaled, to remind us even more that this is a play about nomadic life. The costumes and props come out of them. The boys sleep in them. The family eats off

The backstage dressing room, where an on-end trunk becomes a doorway.

The hotel suite, with one suitcase large enough for the boys to sleep in.

them. The girls perform on top of them. They become doors and hall-ways and just about anything else the script demands.

And at the end, when she has nothing else left, Mama Rose pulls one last thing out of all of them: her name in lights, five feet tall.

"Mama's Turn," with her name inside every suitcase in marquee lights.

Damn Yankees

Americana as apple pie

What a nearly perfect show this is—and what a charmer to design. Written by George Abbott, with music and lyrics by Adler and Ross and choreographed by Bob Fossee, in that glorious postwar era that brought us such musical wonders as *West Side Story, Pajama Game, Kiss Me Kate, Guys and Dolls*, and countless others, *Damn Yankees* is a cleverly wrought tribute to our national pastime—but with a little moral lesson at the same time. And, like *The Crucible*, it's a show that somehow rings truer now than when originally written, particularly in these days of congressional investigations into steroid use and the "success at any price" that seems to permeate all professional sports. (It's an interesting irony that, because of his ill-gained baseball skills, Joe plays for the Washington Senators.) Applegate (what a wonderful character name) might as well offer Joe a syringe as a means of reclaiming that lost youth of his. Instead, Joe gets Lola. Not a bad trade, you understand, but as Joe finds out, the aftereffects are pretty much the same.

This production was on the same minifacility as the one used for *Singing in the Rain*, so once more I was saddled with a small thrust, a vicious overhang, no wings, and no flies. There was some storage down the hall offstage right, but it meant everything had to placed in offstage storage with almost ruthless precision. More importantly, because of the sprawling nature of the work, this was another case where less was definitely more—the Hardy living room was suggested by little more than an angled door panel, a sofa, and a small TV set on a wheeled cart. The same sofa, with a fast recover, did double duty in Applegate's apartment, whose own door panel mirrored Joe's save in complementary colors. Stylistically, the design looked to the wild tail-fin angles and exotic curves of the early 50s, except on the baseball field, whose straight lines indicated that, there, it was all business.

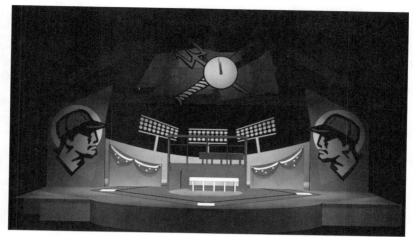

Dugout.

The palette was highly restrictive—as a celebration of America and baseball, literally everything was red, white, and blue. The only variants allowed were the introduction of purple and yellow in Applegate's apartment and desaturated reds and blues in Hardy's home (to suggest

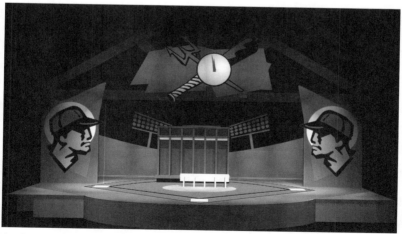

Locker room.

the age of the house), but everything else was bright and almost insanely colorful, with intensely red lockers and a screaming blue bat barrel. You'd think that such a relentlessly pure color scheme would be aggravating after a while, but it was tempered with enough black in the backdrop and white in the furniture and props that everything else—costumes and lighting—could play off those two primaries successfully.

Calamity Jane

a cartoon study in white and blue

Originally a nineteenth-century vaudeville house, the proscenium at this facility is twenty feet wide and twelve feet from deck to ventilator shafts. There's enough of a forestage to allow for small playing areas left and right. And that's pretty well it: barely enough space for a living-room set, and we were to mount a big musical.

From the start, I wondered if there was something conceptually we could do with this piece. Truth be told, it's not a very well-written script. The first act finale doesn't really give us much reason to return for act two: there's no tension for the intermission. And worse, for a romantic musical comedy, Calamity switches her affections from the lieutenant to Bill awfully fast and without a whole lot of preamble. It's just a big ol' cartoon stage adaptation of a big ol' cartoon movie.

That started me thinking in terms of cartoons, especially the way they were styled around 1953, the year the movie was released. Because the stage is so low, I decided to push the idea of the Dakotas' big sky country by creating a backdrop of rotating panels that were painted a brilliant blue with thin little white clouds scudding across: these panels would allow us to move wagons on from upstage (since there was no possible way we could use the nonexistent wings). The panels on the side stages folded against the wall to reveal the Chicago set. A few small cutouts of mountains were placed about the stage to enhance that sense of "big sky," as well as hide a few lighting units. The various set pieces—the bar, the town street, the cabin—were all built in 50s-style skeletal scenery, keeping them compact and tightly expressive.

The basically cartoonish look of the architecture came from another Western musical of that era, *Red Garters*, a bizarre little film (recently released on DVD and well worth checking out) shot entirely on a soundstage, with open framework sets that suggested the town rather

The side panels fold out to reveal architecture in Chicago.

than delineating it. Every scene was bathed in an acid wash of Techni-color, but our approach would be much simpler. Here, practically everything was painted white with only the occasional bit of color, giv-ing the production an almost fairy-tale innocence. In contrast, Calamity's cabin was an uncontrolled gathering of red and green and purple and orange, the first time such pure, intense colors were used. But as Calamity and Katie clean the place (during the aptly named number, "A Woman's Touch"), the cabin ultimately reverts to the same white as the rest of the show, a comic, yet telling moment in which Calamity is more or less "tamed" back into society, if just momentarily.

Beyond making a statement about the rules in Calamity's world, this also serves as an example of using color to solve some inherent problems in the script, for example, the sudden, almost hasty, romance between Bill and Calamity. As noted, there's nothing to telegraph it. It's almost like she's on the rebound—until we start looking at their story from a simple color perspective.

We've already established white as the color representing civiliza-tion, so let's push the conceit a little further. Let's say we reserve white for costuming those who have completely embraced the idea of refined society: Adelaide, Hugh, Danny, and Miller. The general townspeople of Deadwood aren't completely there yet, so we see them in paler, more

Prior to its reappearance in all white, the cabin is a mad splash of color.

muted colors and soft gray-toned pastels—faded denim blue, unsaturated earth tones, and so on—but with enough white in shirts and blouses and accessories that we can see the aspirations to big city life.

Then we see Bill and Calamity, the wild children who wear brightly beaded leather coats. There's a huge turkey feather in Bill's hat band. Calamity's boots are heavily and vividly embroidered. (All of this would

The stagecoach, with wheels made from truncated hoola-hoops.

also give an interesting twist to the fabric that Calamity brings Susan in the first scene: its wild colors are something that of course would attract her, whereas Susan would look at it more askance.) If we visually portray Bill and Calamity as outsiders right from the beginning, the audience can be led to the inevitability of their romance without feeling like "oh yeah, right." This of course gives a whole new level of meaning to Calamity wearing white (or not) to her wedding, but the symbolism is truly too good to pass on.

(And you thought you were just gonna get some simple design to play with; instead, you get a discourse on color theory as it applies to symbolic social strata—yikes!)

Calamity Jane proves that it's possible to take a sprawling, big work and whack it down to a manageable size without shortchanging the audience or compromising the material. Instead of tons of scenery, a few wagons easily sketch the needed ideas and allow the stage to open up and breathe. Instead of racks of costumes, most in the chorus need only change a few accessories because theirs is the simple, unchanging look of a community. It demonstrates the myriad possibilities available when distilling a show rather than just simplifying it and, in that process, allows you to find a unique and stylish vision.

Grease

45-rpm records and a giant Dixie cup

I just did *not* want to do yet another typical production of *Grease*. This would be the fourth time I'd designed the show, and the standard platform and jukebox arrangement, which everybody wants, was getting old.

So, with the director's permission, I allowed myself to woolgather a bit. Let's say this show was actually done in the 1950s and that all the singles we know so well had been released on 45s. That led to the image of a teenage girl's bedroom, where she and her friends play these 45s over and over (and over) while they talk about boys and drink sodas from the local drive-in.

And there it was: a giant 45-rpm record player with a real turntable on top. A big Dixie cup sitting on top of a stack of records. Where would Greased Lightning come from? The front of the record player would swing up like a garage door, and the car would drive out from

The basic set.

Greased Lightnin', entering from inside the phonograph.

inside it. And what to do with the giant cup? Let it also revolve, to transform into a shell that houses the Beauty School Dropout Teen Angel. Huge angular drops of period cars and 50s ephemera redefined the space for every scene and gave the production an over-the-top sensibility that underscored the overscaled scenic units.

This was definitely not a "tiny budget" production by any stretch.

The drive in.

Some of the design elements had to be cut for budget purposes. It has levels, which directors love, and it has lots of moving eye candy, which audiences love, but most importantly, it demonstrates that you can divorce yourself from the standard *Grease* set if you want to.

But only you can make that choice.

Choose wisely. Please.

Straight Plays

Our Town

a disk floating in space

Set in a deep blue box and very much a design precursor of both *Carousel* and *The Crucible*, this approach to Grovers Corners is a raked green disk that revolves to a new position with every act. There are a

The wedding scene.

few additional set pieces—some furniture, an inset platform—but the green disk floating in space defines the look overall. There are two doors—one left, one right—whose symbolism might not be all that obvious until you establish that one is just for entrances while the other is just for exits.

The church in act two is suggested by ringing the disk with chairs for the congregation, giving it a feeling of "people around the world." Those same chairs are inserted into the disk for the cemetery in act three.

I'm not sure why, but raking the disk rather than leaving it flat makes the concept sing a little more. I tried it both ways, and with it level, it was just a playing space. Rake it, and it takes on a very distinct personality: a world on the verge of spinning out of control but never quite doing so.

Hedda Gabler

the zoo story

Inspired by a passage in Irene Corey's wonderful book *Mask of Reality*, this takes Ibsen's heroine and puts her on display as the trophy wife she is.

In the old days of zoos, such as those from Ibsen's time, the cages were small, dark, and incredibly depressing: I can still remember walking through the Central Park Zoo in the mid-1970s and seeing animals in little dark gray concrete boxes with sad expressions that said they'd rather be anywhere than there. The living environment was rarely more than some straw and a box to climb on and maybe a tire suspended by a rope. Before we got smart about it, you could put a stick or a cane or even a hand through the bars to pet that poor little lion, but you risked getting it bitten off.

Hedda's home as a zoo cage.

So it is with Hedda's cage. It's a pretty cage, to be sure: all soft, autumnal colors that make everything deceivingly bright and cheery. It's almost open air, providing that illusion of freedom and escape; you might think it was a porch or a veranda. But it's still a cage, with only the most minimum of furnishings—and even the furniture has the vague suggestion of having been put there for Hedda's amusement, not for practicality: it's the Scandinavian version of the tire and the box. People don't enter this house; they walk past the bars of Hedda's cage, then come in. And once in, they too risk getting bit.

Dominating the set (but placed safely outside) is the portrait of her uncle, here played by Ibsen himself.

The Real Thing

Sheridan redux

Tom Stoppard's play about the people in transitional relationships is, as all Stoppard plays are, a magnificent piece of layout and construction. Scenes will unfold and then later repeat themselves virtually verbatim with different characters, and it's easy to lose yourself in the sheer theatricality of what is, at its most essential, a soap opera. One might even call *The Real Thing* a twentieth-century Restoration comedy of manners.

Because it all moved with such stately and mannered pacing. I opted for a design that likewise would be relentlessly restrained while simple to transform as the play moves from apartment to train car to rehearsal hall to another apartment yet again. It is also a play about maintaining perfect balance at all times, so the symmetry of the set was

The basic set, with its Restoration doors and "inner stage," where wagons literally drifted from one scene to the next.

crucial: everything had to mirror and yet mean something in the very act of doing so, and not just in the sense of everything onstage left has a counterpart on stage right. Those pieces—whether chairs or vases—carried additional layers of symbolism in evoking characters, whether suggesting past lovers or the degree of openness in the current relationship, and the combination of symmetry and symbolism gives the play an "emotional intellectualism" that I think Stoppard would approve of.

The Real Thing is arguably one of the subtlest designs I've ever done, with quiet allusions to "inner stages" and Restoration-style doors left and right, as well as the meticulousness with which the furniture is placed on the stage. It's not as sculptural as the technique applied in The Crucible, as that particular production was designed to speak of the community, not the characters. Here, we use that same spatial geometry to talk about our quartet of shifting husbands and wives and lovers, which makes this design one in which the positioning of things telegraphs, in faint ways, how the drama will play itself out. And in the end, we're brought back full circle to the beginning, but with one very important change in the presentation; a slight one, but one that speaks louder than a Jerry Herman title number.

Harvey

a world gently shaken, never stirred

I love this play, unabashedly so. The movie is one of my top 10 favorites (probably ranking somewhere around number 3), a film I watch on a biennial basis as a reminder of Elwood P. Dowd's gentle mantra (and, again, I paraphrase):

> *My mother used to say, Elwood—she always called me Elwood—she used to say, Elwood, you can either be oh so smart or oh so nice. I've been smart. I recommend nice.*

There is little in any self-help book to equal the simple wisdom of that line: a view I take because through folly and shortsightedness I have violated the spirit of it more times than I care to admit. But this tender comedy about a man who sees an invisible, six-foot white

The parlor.

The rest home.

rabbit is in desperate need of a major revival, so all of us can be reminded that it's better to be nice than smart.

You can say the same for the script: it's definitely nice. The characters are all cartoons, but gentle ones—there is nothing mean or vicious about their various relationships with Elwood. Instead, it's as though none of them knows quite where they stand with him. His world is confidently resolute, while theirs has the reactionary ground perpetually shifting about under their feet. As such, I set this play on a rectangular platform that pivots around a point downstage center; atop it are four simple yet massive columns that themselves rotate to indicate whether we're in Elwood's home or the asylum office. A few pieces of furniture and two wall flats are all that are needed to indicate the scenes, but I added two ladder-back chairs on the actual deck for Elwood and Harvey, giving them a solid footing denied everyone else in the play.

There's also a little piece of whimsy thrown in for good measure: a rigged header line, made from one-inch plastic tubing, that can change from gentle, homey curves to institutionally hard right angles as we move from the house to the office. Almost a delicate reminder of the fey presence of Harvey himself, the header line would, in the final scene, twist into two elongated loops.

Hay Fever

life as art

The family members that wreak havoc in *Hay Fever* are all self-described artistes: authors, painters, musicians, poets. They live what they think are artistically cutting-edge lives, perpetually onstage in bright colors, and they are determined, no matter what, to be the Next Big Thing. At the same time, even though they're obsessed with being "free spirits," they're very regimented about it all. You cannot cross the border of their right to freedom without borders. Under the witty madness lies a foundation made of iron, all controlled havoc.

So rather than the usual, fussy country house, this is a modernist's idea of Heaven. The walls are expanses of bright Mondrian yellow and white. The furniture pieces are the latest things from New York and Paris, designed by name architects like Wright. A painting by that newly

discovered sensation Picasso hangs on one wall above a Constructivist fireplace, and the stairs to the second floor are so light that they almost self-support. This is a house about being chic and daring and iconographic while also clueless about how silly it all is. Yet, outside, the lawn has gone to weeds, and there are no doors, as if to say that as long as they're inside their perfect little bubble, nothing can ever, ever go wrong.

The Importance of Being Earnest

deeper down the rabbit hole

Earnest is a preposterously theatrical play, no bones about it. If you can't come up with a set as irrationally civilized as the script, there's no hope. Turn in your card at the door on the way out.

It seems this mad little farce shines best when you allow the audience to enter into the spirit of things with as much élan as the characters. So let them. For this production, rather than have the enjoyment hand-fed like so many bonbons, the director, the technical director, and I chose to provide a full evening's entertainment that went beyond the pithy lines and emphasized the absurdity in our best Alice-in-Wonderland style. So we came up with a truly white-rabbit, harebrained scheme.

Earnest is about duplicity, people with secret lives, and multiple identities. On one level, they are characters in a play put on for their

Preset, with the curtain down.

The act-one bachelor flat.

own amusement, and at the same time, the real actors in the production itself are, by necessity, pretending to be people they aren't for the audience's amusement. We wondered if there wasn't some way to explore this level upon level of interaction, both between the characters

The act-two garden.

The act-three parlor.

and between the actors and the audience—in effect, something that would mirror the play back on itself.

Upon arrival, audience members were given either yellow or purple tickets, handed out more or less indiscriminately. Fifteen minutes before curtain, all holders of the purple tickets were asked to come to the door. They were escorted in, and the doors closed once more. Then, five minutes before curtain, the yellow ticket holders were invited in. They entered the space (an eighty-by-sixty black box) to find a little proscenium arch with a little red curtain and a slightly thrust set—and banks of empty theatre seats. The play began with the butler coming onto the thrust while someone played an offstage piano. Then, the curtain rose, and there were the purple ticket holders facing the yellow ticket holders, sitting in seats the mirror image of the yellow ticket holders' seats. Suddenly, an expected proscenium play became an unexpected in-the-round one. Those on the purple side were also able to see the backstage, adding yet another layer to the convoluted relationships presented on "stage."

(We were very careful not to let these two worlds collide. Wilde doesn't need gimmickry. Instead, we utilized a few small offstage moments and the set changes to convey what we wanted about life in the theatre.)

Then, in act two, the action started moving out into the audience, with characters walking through the rows of seats (always being careful to say "excuse me" as they passed) and performing entire scenes at the top of the stairs that led down to the audience seating, which transformed the production yet again into an environmental one. We pushed it even further in act three, when Jack's frenzied search for the handbag went completely around the far walls of the theatre, in the darkness behind the seats, in an orchestrated aural frenzy of crashes and pratfalls that no one could see.

Euerybodye

DeathTV

Eventually, at some point in your career you will be asked to design something that demands a knowledge of computer technology. I'm not talking about light plots or construction drafting here; rather, this is in the realm of computer-generated projection work, sound design, film editing—that sort of thing. I've always been hands-on when it comes to these infernal machines, so the possible problems are things I can see coming. But the preproduction of *Euerybodye* pushed everything to a higher, more precipitous level.

Based more or less on the medieval mystery play *Everyman*, this script was adapted as a commissioned piece by a university professor in conjunction with the show's director. It follows essentially the same storyline: someone about to die has to come to grips with her mortality. There are the metaphorical characters representing parts of the

The soundstage set, with the green-screen platform seen at lower left.

A photo from the actual production, showing the green-screen stage in operation.

about-to-be-deceased's life, such as Wisdom, Strength, and so on—except that in this version, names were updated, popular cultural references were added, and the play was given a framework that suggested it was a game show of some kind.

(To be blunt, the script was a mess, with no consistent vision. Sometimes dryly witty, sometimes *Saturday Night Live*, it almost desperately wanted to be "cool," in rhymed couplets and mock Olde English. The original's WyseMan became, for reasons never completely clear, Yogi BareAll, a Sufi into baseball. Yoko Ono figured heavily—and inexplicably—during Euerybodye's final moments. Despite mentions of Paris Hilton and Jerry Springer, the references felt a generation or two out of date. In short, it was the dreaded "original play.")

Having no design brief but an inalterable and quickly looming production schedule, I dove in and hoped for the best. There was the reference to a game show in the prologue, but the concept never went anywhere: it was just a reason to punt the story into motion. Still, it was clear we had something that wanted to make comment about pop culture and mass media—while we're watching this girl prepare to die. It was almost like the type of reality show one might find on the DeathTV Network.

Ah-hah! So why not design it as one? Pursuing the idea further, why not treat the show's studio setting, a reflection of the real world, as the "body," while Euerybodye herself becomes the "spirit"?

To that end, our black box space was transformed into a fully operational TV soundstage, under the premise that our audience was watching a "live" broadcast. We gave it all the trappings: three live-feed cameras (two of which were handheld and could follow the actors around the stage as well as outside the building), banks of monitors, and a small green-screen stage placed opposite the show's main set, whose quasi-Gothic arches and gold-leaf paint work were reminders of the play's medieval roots. There were omnipresent technicians: camera crews, stagehands, and and *a vista* engineer who could switch from one camera shot to another. There were close to forty minutes of computer-generated film work, including the "opening credits," animated backgrounds for the green-screen sections, and the representation of

LyfeFors. The animation used off-the-shelf models, handled in a style that was kept impressionistic and indistinct.

God—or, as she was known here, Lyfe-Fors. As the play progresses, the studio, a marvel of integrated technology, "dies," finally shuttering down at the end to a few spotlights amidst rows of now-dead monitors and abandoned cameras.

The costumes, on the other hand, were much more stylized, as befitting the metaphorical characters wearing them. Spun from Japanese anime and manga, those representing Euerybodye's life were bright, colorful, quirky, and pointedly shallow, while those closer to her death were darker and simpler in form.

There is an upside and a downside to a technology-heavy production. The upside is that such rich eye candy is relatively cheap, and what you can't buy can

Our show's host, Dethe.

Euerybodye's cousin, Handout.

Handout's son, Gimme.

be borrowed or rented—and even then for extremely low rates (in the end, we used about half our projected build and materials budget). The downside is that it takes not only a great deal of preproduction work but a commitment to long techs. The five minutes of the God-in-Heaven animation required a week to finalize the basic character and the rendering technique, followed by three all-nighters to rotoscope frame by frame from rehearsal video before assembling these several thousand frames to create the final film. There were serious fears that we wouldn't be able to combine the green-screen camera, the background animations, the live-feed cameras, and the rear projector into the same master editing console. The onstage camerapeople's movements had to be choreographed, a necessary chore mysteriously left until the very end, which aggravated already heavily frayed nerves. Somehow it all came together, a celebration of style heavily slathered over minimal substance—and maybe that's what modern life truly is.

Hautie (or Beauty in the original).

Jacques (a pun on "jock").

The Shape of Things

a life constantly on display

Neil Bute's play begins and ends in a museum, so it didn't take long to see where I had to go scenically. Each scene builds on its predecessor: one more element is added to change the main character—his appearance as well as his life. He loses weight, he gets some new clothes and a bit of plastic surgery. All these superficial changes ultimately give way to large-scale alterations to his love life and his choice of friends. And at the end, we find that it's all just another museum display.

As such, even though the play wanders here and there, to loft apartments and coffee shops and the lawn outside a building at New York University, we never leave the museum. We simply start with a statue at center stage and then add things as the scenes progress. A café counter becomes a display case. A bed becomes an installation piece.

The final exhibition, with scenic pieces that have been progressively added throughout the evening.

The park scene.

Everything becomes art. And in the middle, guarded by a security rope, high above everything else onstage, a Greek statue of a male nude, an unreachable goal representing unattainable perfection.

(The Greeks had this crazy idea that if you couldn't match perfection, you should at least know what it looks like. We do the same thing today. No surprise.)

Something else emerged when I looked at this design again about three years after the production. At the beginning of the play, it's just the statue. By final curtain, the stage is filled with stuff—journals, large photos, a clothes mannequin, a TV camera and monitor, a bed, display cases, and the statue. Rather than walk away from it, our male lead sits in the middle of all that stuff and watches himself on video, just as he's apparently chosen to abandon the simplicity of his former life for the piles of useless things (and ideas) that come with his new one. I wish I'd realized this when I was designing the play; it would have been a concept worth pursuing further.

(Y'know, actually, looking at the design, it probably is in there.)

Help Wanted

waiting, waiting, waiting

Sometimes it's not a matter of cutting down the scenic requirements. Sometimes you have to go the other way: amplifying them so the play can take on a little style and character. *Help Wanted* is one of those large-cast, easy-demands plays that are custom written for middle and high schools. It uses about twenty-five to thirty actors and is presented as a series of vignettes about finding a job, taking on financial responsibilities—in general, learning to become an adult.

The problem is, the set as described asks too little of the production. This is an example where it is indeed possible to underdesign if you follow the author's vision. Presented in a more or less revue format, no single vignette lasts more than a page or two, so it's important that you have maximum flexibility in the presentation. To address that, the script mandates only blocks, which can be quickly reconfigured into a number of suggested scenes.

That's fine but, in my humble opinion, far too facile a solution. I wondered if we couldn't push the idea a little more without taxing the resources. The play revolves around waiting: waiting to become an adult, waiting to get past the interview, waiting to make money so you can go out and have fun. And certainly one thing we all encounter early on in our working lives is that antiseptic, one-size-fits-all waiting room. The numerous chairs, the large, plinthlike tables, and the sad little artificial plants would allow plenty of ways for transforming the space, and yet we would always be conscious of the real-world environment the kids are confronting at this stage in their lives.

Opera

The Marriage of Figaro

a windup opera

The space for this production is incomprehensibly small, a square about sixteen feet to a side. No wings. No flies. Not even an orchestra pit: an onstage pianist stuck back in one corner provides the accompaniment. The only access offstage is a metal double door upstage center and two doors down left and right that lead, respectively, outside and

into the reception hall. For obvious reasons, the company uses a reduced chorus, but they mount their operas virtually full length. It's a
toy space for a theatre, let alone an opera company.

So if it's a toy space, why not make it a toy production? Using design elements from nineteenth-century German toy theatres, I created
a little windup world where a flick of the wrist sets the plot in motion,
like the clockwork figures that emerge when the hour strikes.

Figaro has four sets: three rooms and a garden. Since the stage was
so small, I opted to follow the sense of the space and started with a free-
standing proscenium (that allowed a couple of more places for entrances and exits), a few miniflats, and some well-chosen pieces of
furniture. The garden was a cut drop that rolled down, olio-style, from
behind the false proscenium. It was an approach that suited the scale
of this little domestic comedy in this little performing space, and the
toy theatre aspects of the design fell right in line.

Mefistofele

heavenly smoke and mirrors

This was the first draft, based on simply listening to the opera and reading the synopsis. In short, it's the Faust story, but it goes from Heaven to Hell and everywhere else in between. A massive phantasmagoric, it makes heavy demands on the design team if Bioto's actual stage directions are followed. Besides traveling through time and space and back again, it's just the sheer scale of the thing that makes it so daunting. The opening scene in Heaven stretches on and on with gorgeous choral work before we see Faust in his study, a street fair, Margarite's garden, Hell, ancient Greece, and finally a prison cell where everyone (except, of course, Mefistofele) is redeemed and gets to live happily ever after. Well, sorta.

So much of the opera revolves around shifts—in time, in space, in characters. I kept seeing a landscape that would have its own sense of

Margarite's garden.

shift, one where things are never quite what you think they are because you're never quite sure what you're seeing. Likewise, I wasn't quite sure how I was going to accomplish that, but I knew it was essential to the success of the production.

This isn't Gounod's *Faust*, not by a long shot. This version is more an elegiac fantasia on the legend than a simple retelling. Bioto almost seems determined to tell you, right at the start, that Faust isn't going to get what he really wants out of this life—and yet at the same time, neither will Mefistofele. It's presented as a celestial shell game, one that's all smoke and mirrors.

That thought sparked a vision of Heaven that was also smoke and mirrors, a small chorus made somehow huge by infinite reflections, a place that was part fun house, part madhouse. But how best to portray that? Mirrors weren't really practical because in order for them to work, the reflections have to be strictly controlled. In a theatre, where every audience member has a slightly different view of the stage, that kind of control is almost impossible. But might there be something else that might work?

Plexiglass. Shifting panes of plexiglass that would allow the reflections I wanted without obstructing the audience's view, and if the panes are constantly in motion, the reflections would move with them. I did

The sheets of plexiglass create a myriad chorus.

Faust's study, where the plexiglass now slides to become doors and walls.

a small computer test of the Heaven scene with a chorus of ten, and the effect was precisely what I hoped: suddenly the stage was filled with a chorus of fifty. An audio simulation revealed another fascinating aspect: as the panes were opened and closed, the different escape avenues provided for the sound gave it a disorienting, neither-here-nor-there effect. This wouldn't be a scene where the chorus just stands there and sings. Instead, the audience would be looking at the stage and have no idea what they were seeing—precisely the effect I wanted.

That accomplished, it was time to see if this would work for the rest of the opera. How should these panes be set to best advantage for the study or the garden? For the study, they became a layered wall that would partially disguise Mefistofele's first appearance by refracting him. In the garden, they allowed for an effect similar to that in Heaven: Mefistofele's pursuit of Martha would be visually jumping all over the stage.

Tales of Hoffman

caged by memory

There are times when a particular material just sits there and says, "Use me!" When it's a particular material that's also relatively cheap and readily available, then its employment becomes irresistible.

With *Hoffman*, I wanted something that would suggest the drunken fog of memory, but in a less obvious way than scrim cloth. This isn't a "scrim" opera: Hoffman's visions aren't the cloudy, soft-focus images of loves long past. They're angry and hostile and petulant. Even as he declares his love, he's got some sort of chip on his shoulder about it because I think he knows, even as he's saying it, that it won't work out. Fate is completely against him. The girl will leave him or die or get disassembled or something. Yet at the same time he also knows that he's trapped by these same reveries. In every case (if you use traditional casting), it's the same woman. In every case, it's the same man standing

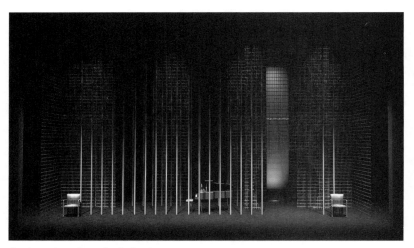

A piano in a forest of steel.

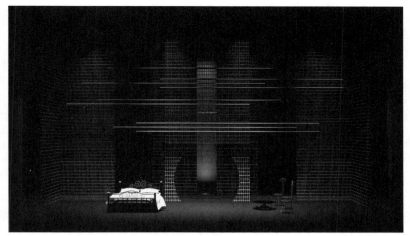

A Venetian bed with an audience.

between him and her. Even in the end, when he thinks he'll finally get his chance, he misses out yet again, and you know that were we to see *Tales of Hoffman: The Sequel*, that actress would get an act of her own so he could tell us all about her.

Because of its inherent ability to reflect light, layered steel mesh has a perplexing, nonspecific look; you're not quite sure which layer you're looking at, let alone how many layers there might be. It's difficult to know how far upstage someone is when they walk through the stuff. And all of this gives a steel-mesh construction a wonderfully vague yet hard-edged and almost hostile feel.

The design also has a cut-out moon gate that shifts from one side to the other and a suspended array of steel tubing that arrives horizontally, vertically, or at odd angles, depending on which act we're watching. Finally, the look is completed with rich, modern furnishings, including a Venetian bed that comes with its own silent voyeurs.

Madama Butterfly

the island kingdom of the soul

Even in operatic terms, there is a haunting simplicity to the music of *Madama Butterfly*, one that is best performed when the staging is as understated as a tea ceremony. Lavishness and pomp work against this essentially little tragedy.

At the same time, one has to deal with the huge expanse of the opera stage, which means that, like a Japanese sumi painting of a circle, the message is best conveyed in sweeping gestures of great economy: if your heroine is celebrating the return of her long-absent husband by decorating the house with flowers, we should see flowers everywhere. And yet, with Japanese élan, these are flowers that manifest through their own innate simplicity, petals of pure color falling through the skies.

The "Flower Song," with a scrim drop of stylized flower petals of blood red.

The finale, under a setting sun.

It is not out of convenience that Butterfly's story takes place on a hill overlooking the ocean. True, this is where she can see Pinkerton's ship, but also there is something about the shore that suggests finality, the last bit of ground before the invisible depths of the ocean—and by extension then, the last bit of connection to her past as she faces an uncertain future.

So what we have here is the collision of the Floating Kingdom that is Japan with the Soul Cut Adrift that is Butterfly. Her life is played out on a series of islands that, on one hand, represent Japan's image of itself and, on the other, represent Butterfly's own image of herself. Abandoned because of her choice and finding that it was the wrong one, she tries to drop anchor back home, only to find out, as we always do, that you can't go home again.

Played before a triple layer of dead hung scrim, the design also uses a few abstract flown pieces—the square flowers and the horizontally striped sun—to reaffirm its oriental heritage. A very simple approach that allows us yet again to concentrate on the characters, not the production.

Così Fan Tutte

reflections on mirror images

Yes, this is that tired "rehearsal room" cliché that directors like to use on occasion when they can't think of anything else to do. But what serves it well here is that it allows the audience to see outside the opera a bit. We have characters that adopt disguises and push their lives into fun-house mirror reflections of themselves, so why not push that thought to another level?

And the giant rehearsal mirror itself, reflecting not only the world of the opera but the audience as well. Yes, done to death, but here, it takes a different spin because it's set at an angle that allows only a part of the audience to be seen within. We're part of the opera and yet not: we sit on the sidelines of the reflection, not center stage.

Turandot

Puccini, Hammer-timed

Puccini's last opera customarily evokes a delirium of unstudied excess. One has only to look at the Metropolitan Opera's utterly over-the-top version to see how the traditionalists prefer their Chinoise princesses who kill anyone who says, "I love you."

But that storyline—gads. A kingdom where time has effectively come to a standstill in some weird eternal night. A revenge-driven princess whose blood lust is one step away from sheer petulance. A chorus of her dead victims, warning the prince to get out and get out fast, except that he's so blinded by her beauty that he can't think of anything else—even to the point of ignoring the one woman who loves him for himself. The famous riddle scene, that psychological tennis match, where love truly means nothing and everything is about power and control. Face it: this is a sick little horror story, as macabre and twisted as anything from Hammer Studios in its prime.

(If you haven't seen the recent production that uses the "new" ending, you're missing something that accentuates how disturbing this opera can be. In it, Liù dies by her own hand, but now the body remains on the stage. Turandot and Tamil sing to each other over it, as though the corpse were just another piece of furniture. Yikes.)

So let's make it a haunted house, with an act-one city gate and an act-two throne room that's covered with dust and decay and operatically scaled spiderwebs, something truly terrifying in all its self-indulgent glory. In the act three garden, there's not just one moon, but a whole host of them, bearing the faces of Turandot's many victims. An empty, desolate place of broken stone statuary. A color palette of desaturated blues and purples and decayed wood tones, creating a relentlessly icy,

The Great Hall, covered with dust and huge spiderwebs.

somber atmosphere that finally releases in a blaze of color and light as we celebrate the power of love.

But does Turandot really love Tamil, as she says? Not a chance. It's not love; it's flat-out lust, a carnal passion that comes from dominance and submission. The man on top got there by momentarily relinquish-

The home of the advisers, Ping, Pang, and Pong.

ing control to her in a psychological crapshoot. In the process, he beat her at her own game, and that turns her on like nothing she's felt in, well, apparently quite a long time, given the number of heads on pikes she keeps around the palace's front door. It's a poker strategy, and I give this marriage six months, tops, before she decides to add his to the collection.

A Final Suggestion

Unless IT'S A TOURING PRODUCTION OF *Phantom of the Opera* or *Les Miz*, theatre by its very nature is an ephemeral art form.

And thank goodness for that.

I've designed (as of this writing) over two hundred productions in eight countries on three continents. While I'm proud of my work on every single one, I know as well as I'm sitting here that there are a few genuine clunkers in my portfolio. Much as we parents might wish otherwise, not all of our children grow up to be the prettiest or the smartest or the most successful. Some of them are early designs, when I was still finding my artistic feet, so to speak. Others were simply creative misfires that should have been stopped dead in the conceptual process. I never see it at the time, of course; it's not until a year or two passes and then I look back and I say to myself, "Self, what the heck were you thinking?" Maybe it was a color, or a texture, or a shape—but whatever it was, it didn't work, and I have no one to blame but myself.

I can live with that.

Any creative professional will tell you: at a certain point, it's time to let go. The novel will never be more perfectly literary than it already is. The painting will never shimmer with more interior light. The poem will never have rhymes more intricate or polished. And, for us, the set and costumes will never be more conceptually brilliant. So finish the job: draft the working drawings, prepare the painters' elevations, select the fabrics and trim, supervise the tech, approve the set dressing, celebrate at the opening night party, and then move on to the next project.

Let. It. Go.

Do not misunderstand here. I'm not saying just give it all up lightly and write it off as a bad blind date. The methods described in this book require more front-end work than anything else, and that's a big investment to put into any job. When you're drawing on as much personal knowledge and research as we designers do, you feel a huge amount of ownership, as well you should. In the beginning, you're not just a designer—you're a director, a dramaturge, a choreographer, a costumer, a lighting designer, a tech director, and an actor, all rolled up in one great big abstract package. But don't misunderstand the purpose of taking on all those hats. It is your job to anticipate to a large degree the decisions made by your partners on the creative team because (as much as they might disagree with this statement) it is your work that binds most of them together. Remember what I said at the outset about design as a good party host? That statement about how the good host knows when to recede into the background? A good host does exactly that, but the host also sets the tone for the party, just as you as a designer set the tone for the performance. You create the world, then everyone else populates it, dresses it up, lights it—in general, makes that world functional. That's the bottom line, absolutely first requirement of any designer: the work has to function. It might be the most brilliant design ever conceived for *Natalie Needs a Nightie*, but if it doesn't function, if they can't use it, then no matter how much you may have invested in it, you're of no use.

That's tough to accept sometimes, but best you hear it now, right?

But here's something equally brutal that needs to be said in corollary: not all your designs will function the way you hoped they would. Despite your best efforts, some will fall flat on their faces (been there), some will limp through the performance like brave little soldiers (done that), some will appear to work just fine then mysteriously disintegrate somewhere around the middle of act two on opening night (got the T-shirt). You'll be tempted to assign blame—to the director, to the lighting director, to yourself. Trust me: that's a classic exercise in futility. Instead, make a note of what went wrong and why and file it away under E for Experience. Then fix the problem as best you can, have a great time at the cast party, and forget about it. Don't worry: file E will still be there when you sober up the next morning.

Let me give you an example. Early in my career, I was contracted by a regional playhouse to design a musical. Complex show with lots of scenes. I worked on that puppy for months, ensuring everything was right—in the design, the drafting, everything. This was a Break: the kind of commission that could lead to bigger and better things, and I didn't want to blow it. I arrived a week before opening to supervise load-in and tech, and I couldn't wait to see my work realized onstage. Everyone in the shop was excited by the designs; it was a radical approach to a tired old show, and there was much anticipation among the cast and crew to see these beauties under lights.

Was I excited? You bet I was.

The problems came when I discovered I only had roughly 70 percent of the needed storage space backstage. The company manager hadn't told me, for example, that most of the upstage left corner was used for flat storage, and that ate a good seventy square feet. All of a sudden, the set I had designed and worked out in infinite detail didn't fit. I had two large wagons, both extremely important design elements, that had no place to live. The shift schedule, which I had worked out in excruciating detail so platform A would be in position to move on as platform B came off, well, that was history as well. To make matters worse, the choreographer decided he needed more space for the show's only dance number, so he unilaterally had the tech director move the show's backdrop upstage five feet, which took out another hundred square feet of storage and maneuvering space. Finally, I had a running crew of two, not the five I had requested. The first tech was a nightmare, putting a serious wedge between the production team and the performers. And my own reaction to this dilemma?

Being stupid, I went ballistic. Blame got tossed around like rice at a Presbyterian wedding. If only the idiot choreographer had left my backdrop alone! If only the stage manager had informed me that there was a pile of flats sitting up left! Didn't anyone look at the drawings when they came in?! Surely someone could have noticed that I had a wagon sitting in the middle of their scenic storage!

And so on and so on.

Not a smart move. Things escalated to the point where I was none too gently asked to leave two nights before opening, and the company (rightfully) never asked me back for another show. Considering how tightly knit the professional theatre community is, that tantrum probably set my career back by a good five years. Looking at the problem now, with twelve years' distance, I can easily see what could have been done to fix it: a couple of scenic elements could have been eliminated; others cut down a little. A little juggling here and there, and it would have been fine.

But, gosh darn it all, I was creating art here.

Or so I told myself.

Now I look back and think, y'know, the morning after the last performance, most of that art wound up in a dumpster.

You have to know when to let go. Of the design, of the construction, of your personal investment in all of it. Two or three weeks from opening night, it won't exist any more.

We designers are in a curious limbo vis-à-vis the production hierarchy. We talk to the director and the tech director and, of course, among ourselves, but we don't get to interact with the cast with the same degree of intimacy as the director. The performers see us at the design presentation, at the costume fittings, and at final techs, but that's it. We might as well be gods descending from Mount Olympus as they grovel on hand and foot before us and—

Wait. We are gods, aren't we?

Well, no. We're just part of the team: the part that sits in the back of the theatre while everyone else is onstage. The press usually forgets us in their reviews, and we rarely get to participate in the curtain calls, but frankly that's how it goes. And maybe for good reason. It's not about us; it's about them—the director and the performers onstage. Trust me, the sets could burn to the ground and the costumes could fall apart in the wash and every spotlight in the building could short out, and the play could still go on. Yes, we build the world they live in, but no one says they have to live there.

Let. It. Go.

So what if the director doesn't understand your amazing concept. So what if the master carpenter didn't follow your specifications to the letter. So what if the costumes look like they belong in a completely different show and the set painting looks as textured as a bowl of week-old milk and the lights make everything look like a scene from *The Wild Duck*.

Let. It. Go.

Maybe the problem is that no one's communicating. Maybe the problem is that the director doesn't know what he wants. Maybe the problem is that your shop crew is understaffed and inexperienced.

Or maybe the problem is that your design just doesn't work.

Let. It. Go.

Even Oliver Smith and Jo Mielziner had their creative gaffes, just as you and I have had and will continue to have. But whatever the problem, whoever's fault it might be, however the problem chooses to manifest itself, just fix it as thoroughly as you can and then move on. You'll get another chance to create art later, I promise. But stopping everything so you can obsess about a failed opportunity and a black mark on your otherwise spotless résumé isn't exactly doing much to deal with the crisis at hand, nor is it likely to win you any professional friends and contacts. If you've otherwise done your job, the audience won't care that the shade of green on the floor cloth isn't exactly right. They won't notice that the dining chairs are upholstered in different fabrics.

Know why?

They'll be enjoying the play.

And isn't that all that really matters? Pleasing all the little people sitting out there in the dark?

So accept now that not everything that springs from your fevered brow will be perfection. As Gwendolyn says in *Earnest* (and I paraphrase), "Oh, I do hope I am not perfect, Mr. Worthing. That would leave no room for improvement."

Now, go design a play.

A TECHNICAL NOTE

The design models seen throughout this book were created in a variety of software (notably Strata and Amapi), then rendered in Bryce3D, on a G5 iMac running OSX 10.3.9. The computer rendered costumes were created in eFrontier's Poser, using both preexisting and custom-made mesh models with textures developed in Adobe Illustrator CS and Photoshop CS.

ABOUT THE AUTHOR

Graphic designer, illustrator, and stage designer, Sean Martin's work has been seen across North America, Europe, and Asia. He has served as resident designer for four companies, worked on a major international premiere in Spain, and donated his services to a score of schools and theatre companies around the world. Directors and critics have hailed his work for its sense of style and concept as well as its distinctive use of color. Author of several articles and a noted lecturer on virtual design, Martin's company At This Stage has pioneered the use of computer technology to combine virtual actors, sets, costumes, speech, music, and choreography into a fully animated in situ preview. Martin was a 2004 semifinalist for the Theatre Communications Group/ National Endowment for the Arts Award for Mid-Career Design.